MEDIEVAL MEDICINE
IN ILLUMINATED MANUSCRIPTS

MEDIEVAL MEDICINE
IN ILLUMINATED MANUSCRIPTS

Peter Murray Jones

THE BRITISH LIBRARY

CENTRO TIBALDI

Original edition first published 1984 under the title
Medieval Medical Miniatures by The British Library
and University of Texas Press

This revised edition first published in 1998 by
The British Library
96 Euston Road
St Pancras
London NW1
by arrangement with Centro Tibaldi, Milan, Italy

ISBN 0 7123 0657 9

British Library Cataloguing in Publication Data
A CIP Record is available from The British Library

Designed and produced by Centro Tibaldi, Milan, Italy
Printed in Italy by Mediagraf, Noventa Padovana (PD)

Front cover:
Florence, Biblioteca Laurenziana, *Gaddi 24, c. 247v*

Back cover:
London, British Library, *Royal MS 15 E II, f. 165*

CONTENTS

ACKNOWLEDGEMENTS

I welcome the opportunity to prepare a slightly revised version of this book, first published in 1984. Thanks go to Centro Tibaldi for this opportunity.

I should like to thank the Wellcome Trustees for help in meeting the costs of colour illustrations for this book, and the Wellcome Institute for permission to reproduce photographs of Wellcome manuscripts, and for the courtesy and helpfulness of the Library staff in the course of many visits over the past three years. I owe a particular debt, like many others, to Dr. Vivian Nutton of the Wellcome Institute for reading through one draft of the book – though he is not in any way responsible for any of the faults that remain. William Schupbach, curator of iconographic collections, and Dr Richard Palmer, curator of Western manuscripts, gave generously of both time and knowledge. Dr Faye Getz, Wellcome Research Fellow, knows as much about medieval English medicine as a student could reasonably ask, and has an office minutes away from the British Museum; not surprisingly she has often been appealed to, and never in vain.

Others have provided help in their own specialised areas of expertise. Dr Ghislaine Skinner of the Wellcome Museum for the History of Medicine at the Science Museum, Mr John R. Kirkup, and Dr. Ralph Jackson of the Department of Prehistoric and Romano-British Antiquities at the British Museum, have all helped answer my enquiries about surgical instruments of the Middle Ages. Professor Linda Voigts, of the University of Missouri, Kansas City, passed on her findings in the Sloane manuscripts and much helpful advice. Dr Kathleen Scott has been kind enough to point out the significance of details of costume worn in the pictures in Sloane MS 6. Dr Brunsdon Yapp shared some of his encyclopaedic knowledge of the birds which appear in medieval manuscripts. Claire Daunton, née Gobbi, has kept up a stream of picture postcards showing scenes from continental manuscripts and paintings, all with a medical theme. It goes without saying that I am also obliged to many authors who cannot be listed here, for information about particular manuscripts, or more generally about medicine and the visual arts in the Middle Ages.

Finally I have to thank my colleagues in the British Library, and particularly the Department of Manuscripts, who have often helped me, without necessarily realising quite how. Derek Turner and Janet Backhouse allowed some of their knowledge of illuminated manuscripts to rub off on me. Others in the British Library have provided encouragement and practical help, among them Elaine Paintin and Jane Lee of the Education Service, Hugh Cobbe, Publications Officer, and Jane Carr, who handled the early stages of the project for this book. David Way, my editor, deserves special thanks for his valuable advice, criticism, and patience. Without the photographs this book would be pointless; I would like to thank the photographic staff of the British Library, particularly Chris McGlashon and Jane Mullane, and of the Wellcome Institute, for accommodating themselves so readily to demands verging on the unreasonable.

Peter Murray Jones

INTRODUCTION

This book is intended to display some of the extraordinary wealth of medical illustration to be found in medieval manuscripts. Most of the illustrations reproduced here are from medical books, designed to be read and used by physicians, or laymen with an interest in the theory and practice of medicine. A few only are from non-medical manuscripts, included because of their medical interest. The artists and draughtsmen of medical books appreciated just as much as we do today the value of pictures in the conveying of certain kinds of information. Pictures could be used to illustrate case-histories, to demonstrate techniques, to make instruments for diagnosis and prognosis, to reveal structures and functions within the body, to depict the substances needed to make medicines, and to do a lot more besides. Because manuscripts are hand-made things, no two pictures are ever the same in point of detail or in quality of execution, even when they were meant to serve the same purpose or belonged to a well-established tradition.

A select handful of the manuscripts shown here are famous because of quality of design and splendour of illumination – these stand out as documents in the history of art, and have often been reproduced. What they have to tell us about medicine has not always been appreciated, and it is this aspect that will be concentrated on here. But most medical illustration was not work of such refinement, and has been ignored by historians of art. These ordinary manuscripts are just as interesting as the select few, because they tell us so much about the role of the book in medieval medicine, and something of what it must have been like to study and practise the healing arts in this period. The reader will be able to see for himself the extraordinary range and diversity in subject-matter and style of these pictures; the chapters of this book aim to provide sufficient information for him to interpret the pictures as documents of medical history rather than of art. Above all, this means looking at the picture not as an isolated object but as an integral part of the manuscript in which it is found. The text or captions which accompany the picture are given particular attention.

The illustrations in this book come from manuscripts in the collections of the British Library, the Library of the Wellcome Institute for the History of Medicine in London, and of some of the great Italian libraries. They represent only a fraction of the pictures which might have been chosen for reproduction from among thousands of medical manuscripts. Many of the manuscripts were acquired by two remarkable collectors, Sir Hans Sloane (1660 – 1753), and Sir Henry Wellcome (1853 – 1936). Sloane, whose collections formed the basis of the British Museum, acquired over 5000 manuscripts, the majority of them medical, from the proceeds of an enormously lucrative career as a fashionable general practitioner. Not all the British Library examples come from the Sloane collection, but his must be the greatest collection of medical manuscripts ever made by a single individual. Sir Henry Wellcome became sole proprietor of the Burroughs Wellcome pharmaceuticals company in 1895, and devoted much of his time and money to amassing medical books and objects, including a substantial collection of medical manuscripts. Neither man concentrated on manuscripts with pictures alone; they were omnivorous, acquiring anything connected with their medical interests.

Not all the illustrations in this book are miniatures in the strict sense of having been created in illuminating workshops. (The term 'miniature' is supposedly derived from the Latin minium, meaning red lead, as used by illuminators.) Many of them are simple outline drawings or diagrams in ink, made by the scribe who wrote out the manuscript. Medical books in medieval times were not just owned as treasures, but were in constant use, both as a means of providing medical education and as sources of important information for reference purposes. The reason why so many of the medical books have survived, despite heavy wear and tear, is that they were copied again and again, by and for those who needed them. The sketches and diagrams in these manuscripts had their own part to play in storing information, because there were occasions when images were much more effective than words.

THE EARLIEST MEDICAL MINIATURES

The earliest medical illustration in this book dates from about 400 AD (see Fig. 50). It is not strictly a medieval manuscript of course, but is included as the best surviving relic of medical illustration in the Hellenistic era. This papyrus, known from its discoverer as the Johnson papyrus, was found at Antinoopolis in Egypt in 1904. It seems originally to have been part of one folio from a codex otherwise lost, whose dimensions must have been about 250 x 160 mm. We may assume, despite the unique nature of this tattered remnant, that in Greek and Roman times medical books of all kinds were frequently illustrated (see Fig. 2). The available literary evidence suggests this; for instance, it seems, from comments by Aristotle, that some of his works on natural history were meant to be illustrated. A great quantity of illustrated medical literature written on papyrus must have disappeared, with only a few fragments of paintings of plants left behind, preserved by the sands of Egypt. Alexandria was the most important centre of medical research and education in the ancient world from the 3rd century BC to the 7th century AD, but nothing is left of this vast storehouse of medical papyri to tell us of its tradition of medical illustration.

If the Johnson papyrus was our only witness, our opinion of Hellenistic illustration might not be very high. But one great codex survives (on parchment) which hints at the lost glories of classical illustration. It contains exquisitely lifelike paintings of plants, birds, snakes, reptiles, and mammals. This is the Juliana Anicia codex, made about 512 AD in Byzantium and now in the Austrian National Library in Vienna. (See Fig. 1.) Its pictures suggest that classical illustration of materia medica (substances of medical value) was far more naturalistic than at any subsequent point before the 15th century. It has been estimated that as much as 40% of the illustration in this book shows some evidence of direct observation of nature. The book also includes a portrait of the famous rhizotomist, or root-cutter, Crateuas. He was doctor to Mithridates VI, King of Pon-

tus c.100 BC, and the author of an illustrated herbal which is supposed to have formed the basis for all later botanical illustration. Some of the pictures in the Juliana Anicia codex may be distant descendants of those in Crateuas's book, and they are our best witness for the character of classical illustration of materia medica. Other branches of medical illustration were carried on in Byzantium, but the examples left to us are much later in date than the Juliana Anicia codex, and further removed in style from the classical.

But if the classical style vanished, classical subjects and conventions did not. We have to thank the copyists, most working in monastic scriptoria (writing workshops), for this continuity; their respect for images handed down from generation to generation ensured the images' survival. When an older model was available, the scribe or illuminator got on with the job of copying. He copied it even when the words and pictures had become so mangled by copying and recopying that he might easily have turned instead to scenes around him, or to the plants and animals he saw every day; yet still he preferred to copy distorted or unintelligible images from the book in front of him. The earliest parchment codex discussed in this book, British Library Cotton MS Vitellius C III (see pp. 61-62) seems at first glance to have been copied with at least half an eye on the natural world. But, although the line cannot be traced, it is in fact the descendant of a long line of previous manuscripts. Many of the cures attributed to the plant and animal recipes in this manuscript are credited, revealingly, to the authority of pagan gods, goddesses, or heroes - Apollo, Mercury, Diana, Aesculapius, Chiron, and Achilles. Monastic scribes seem happily to have accepted these survivors of pagan mythology as medical authorities.

The title page of this Anglo-Saxon manuscript shows its classical ancestry quite clearly. The title reads 'Herbarium Apulei Platonici quod accepit ab escolapio et [-] chirone centauro magistro achillis'; the author of the herbal, mistakenly identified as Apuleius Platonicus, is supposed to have accepted his book (that is, drawn the authority for what

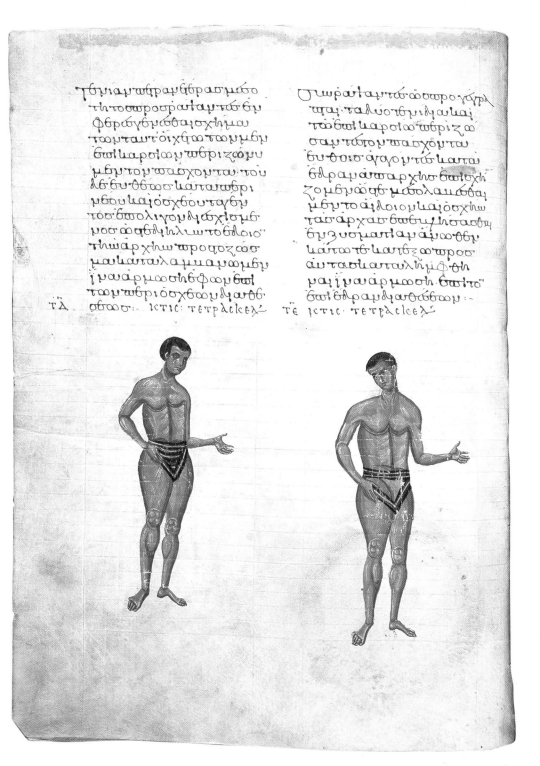

Fig. 2
An 11th-century
Byzantine manuscript
of the *De fasciis*
(On bandages)
of Soranus of Ephesus.
Two patients wearing
trusses are shown.
These illustrations
were not known
or copied in the West
until the 15th century.
*Florence,
Biblioteca Laurenziana,
MS Plut. 74.7, f. 237v*

Fig. 3
Aesculapius, 'Plato', and Chiron.
'Plato' (Apuleius Platonicus), in the centre,
is the supposed author of the herbal from which this
painting comes. Aesculapius and the centaur Chiron,
the master of Achilles, give the book to him and
so confer their authority on it. English, 11th century.
BL, Cotton MS Vitellius C. III, f. 19

he says) from Aesculapius and the centaur Chiron, the master of Achilles. Even the lettering and ring ornament used for the title are similar to those found in the Juliana Anicia codex, five centuries earlier. On another page (see Fig. 3), the author and his authorities themselves are depicted. The author is in the middle receiving the book from the smaller figures, representing Aesculapius on the left and Chiron the centaur on the right. Aesculapius is dressed up in the classical style as a bearded man wearing a chiton and hima-tion. The remains of his customary attribute, the snake-entwined staff, can still be seen between him and the author; the staff itself has been lost, but the snakes are still there. Chiron the centaur carries a skin over one shoulder in a tradition also derived from classical art. So both in words and in pictures this 11th-century manuscript bears witness to its origins in the 4th century AD. The presentation page neatly symbolises the debt owed by medieval medical illustration to its classical origins.

THE END OF A TRADITION

The earliest manuscript sets one limit to the scope of this book, even though we know that the tradition to which it belongs stretches right back to Antiquity. But when and how are we to define the end of the period of medieval medical illustration? At first sight, this question appears easy to answer, because we know that, with the arrival of the printed book, manuscript illustration was doomed to decline. Therefore we might think it is just a matter of determining when the transition from one to the other was complete. There are very few illustrated medical manuscripts from the 16th century, compared with the 15th century, and the post-1500 pictures in this book are special cases of one sort or another. For example, the manuscript written and illuminated for Bishop François de Dinteville in 1525 (Fig. 13) was not a medical manuscript at all, but a luxury private prayer-book. The artist's model book or sampler, which includes a picture of a hernia operation (Fig. 85), dates from the 16th century, but was probably designed to impress a wealthy potential patron with the artist's technical expertise. It is not strictly a medical book, and in any case the artist certainly copied many of its designs from printed books. Only Wellcome MS 93, which contains bloodletting figures (Fig. 88), really counts as 16th century medical illustration, and even there one of those figures is in fact a woodcut, not manuscript at all.

So it looks as if the advent of the printed book in the second half of the 15th century effectively doomed medical illustration in manuscript. In a single pull of the press, woodcuts could be printed alongside the text, and thus duplicated time after time. Even though, in the late 15th century, medical illustrations were still being produced in competition with what was available in printed books, by the mid 16th century the battle had been won by the new technology of movable type and wood blocks.

But there is another way of looking at this change-over in techniques from handwriting to print and woodcut. The medical books printed in the 15th century and first half of the 16th century show a strong allegiance to the manuscript tradition of illustration, publishing the same kinds of text and pictures as had been the staples of manuscript production. Such illustrations as the table of urine glasses, the series of foetal positions in the womb, the zodiac man, and the alphabetical series of medicinal simples, were taken over by the first printed books and given wider currency than they had ever had in manuscript. A good example of this take-over is the wound-man found in Hans Gersdorff's *Feldtbüch der Wundartzney* ('Field Book of Wound Surgery'), published at Strasburg in 1517 (Fig. 4). Compare this with the manuscript wound-man of a century earlier (Fig 84): the pose of the near-naked man is similar, and the range of wounds, abscesses, and sores is the same too. Someone went to the trouble of colouring the woodcut in this particular book by hand, trying to get the same effect as a manuscript illustration. With woodcuts in manuscripts, and hand-colouring in woodcuts, the blurring of technical boundaries is as important a factor as the continuity in subject-matter.

The printers of the first books using movable type even tried to imitate manuscripts in the form of their scripts and decoration, as well as in the illustrations. Their books were simply manuscripts in printed form, and so, unlike manuscripts, reproducible again and again. It was not until authors, illustrators, and publishers began to consider the possibility that printed books and woodcuts might be used to do something altogether different from the manuscript book, that medical illustration itself (the message rather than the medium) underwent radical change. This revolution is usually credited, not without good reason, to Andreas Vesalius, because he saw that a printed textbook could be used in a novel way for teaching human anatomy.

What Vesalius saw was this. While illustrations had necessarily to be copied by hand from one book to another, the more complicated the picture the more likely it was to become corrupt in copying. The sheer mechanics of copying meant also that only a very limited 'edition' of a manuscript book could be produced, thus drastically reducing the potential profitability of an instruction-al manual. Only wealthy, or comparatively wealthy, people could afford illustrated manuscripts. A *de luxe* printed edition, like the *De humani corporis fabrica* ('On the structure of the human body'), containing very large and detailed illustrations, could appeal to the lover of fine books as much as to the eminent professor of medicine. But then Vesalius also published an *Epitome* of the *De fabrica* in the same year (1543), and the smaller work was intended to act as an introduction for the beginner in medicine. Because it was cheaper, the *Epitome* could be run off in an edition of hundreds, or even thousands. Given the assurance that each copy would be as like another as could be, then there was no problem with the corruption of text or illustration, and sufficient numbers could be sold, even to students without much money, to make a didactic work profitable.

The publication of these two books in 1543 marks the point at which we can say that the manuscript tradition of medical illustration really was doomed. But Vesalius's achievement in anatomy was only the most spectacular development of the new illustration. In other fields of medicine there were parallel developments which were just as significant. For example, the first modern botanical illustration dates from as early as 1530-6, when Otto Brunfels's *Herbarum vivae eicones* ('Living pictures of plants') was published at Strasburg. The plants in this book were drawn from nature by Hans Weyditz, as we know from 64 original sketches which were only discovered in 1930. Brunfels's folio herbal, and the *De historia stirpium* ('On the natural history of plants') of Leonhart Fuchs which appeared at Basel in 1542 were followed rapidly by editions in quarto and smaller sizes using the same illustrations, as well as pirated editions which copied them. These brought the book within the reach of the poorer student of medicine and botany, who could compare his own collections and observations directly with the woodcuts in the book.

TEXT AND ILLUSTRATION

With the new didactic sort of medical illustration, text and picture are complementary, working together to promote the aim of understanding structures or elucidating techniques. The relationship between the author of the work and the illustrator is relatively straightforward – the illustrator simply executes the author's intentions under his (or perhaps the publisher's) direction. The reader is left in the role of mere consumer of the finished product, and the author and publisher who venture the book on the market do so in the hope that they have produced the right article, at the right price to attract purchasers.

All these uncomplicated relationships become complicated when we look at the older manuscript illustrations. In the case of each single illustrated medical book in manuscript, questions have to be asked about almost everything we take for granted in printed books. Do the illustrations have anything to do with the text at all, and have text and illustrations always belonged to one another? Were the illustrations intended as mnemonic devices, as pure decoration, as ways of dividing up a text, as diagnostic or prognostic tools, as guides to technique, or as something else again? Who was the illustrator – was he (or they) the scribe or a professional working in an illuminating workshop? Did the author intend his text to be illustrated at all? What did the commissioner or purchaser want, and how did he use the book once complete?

The answers to these sorts of question can only be provided by looking at the illustrations in the context of all the evidence that the text and the physical format of the book have to offer. That can only really be done by examining each example separately. Much of this book will be devoted to these individual enquiries. But there are some things that can be said in general about the circumstances of production of manuscript illustration, whether of the miniature proper, or of pen sketches or diagrams. There is also the intellectual make-up of Western medicine in the Middle Ages to be considered, because this of course had its own part to play in determining what sorts of illustrations were produced, and when. Both these sets of factors will be considered in turn.

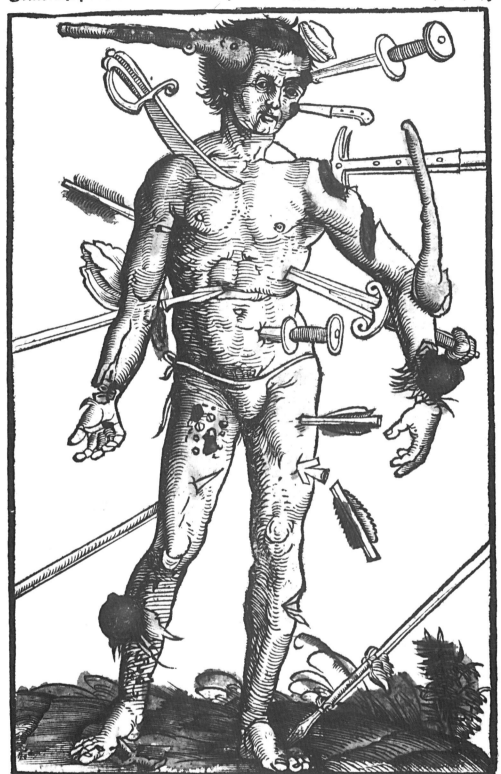

ℂWiewol ich bin voll ſtreich vñ ſtich/ Doch hoff ich gott/ kunſtlich artzney/
Zermorrſcht/verwundet iämerlich/ Schylhans der werd mit helfē frey.

Fig. 4
The wound man shows the variety of wounds, injuries, and external ailments with which a surgeon might have to deal.

From Hans Gersdorff, *Feldtbuch der Wundarztney* (Strasburg, 1517), p.xviii verso. The woodcuts in the British Library copy have been coloured by hand.
BL, Dept. of Printed Books, C.3l m 12

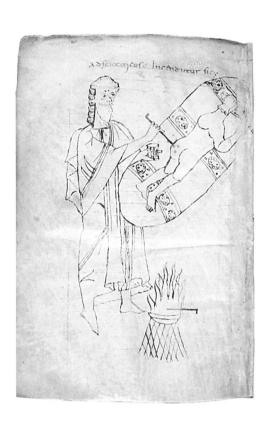

THE MAKING OF MINIATURES

Broadly speaking, medical illustrations in manuscript before the 13th century were mostly the products of monks, writing and painting in monastic *scriptoria*; after the 13th century, they mostly came from lay *scriptoria* and illuminating workshops, or from the pens of private individuals. This implies of course that there was no such thing as a professional medical illustrator. By the 15th century some workshops may have had a special line in medical work, but certainly in what we may call the monastic era of medical illustration, medical manuscripts and their illustrations were made in the same places and by the same people as those who were responsible for bibles, service-books, prayer-books, chronicles, and all the other works of philosophy and literature which the monastic orders thought it their duty to transmit to posterity for the greater glory of God. Their task was one of faithful preservation, but also one of adornment, for to beautify a book was to pay homage to God, an attitude which carried over to some extent from sacred to profane literature.

Monastic illustration of medical books was characterised by respect for the authority of the existing pictorial tradition. From the 6th century onwards the monastic houses were at work copying the books which had survived the collapse of the western Roman Empire. The accidents of survival must have outweighed deliberate choice in determining which sorts of illustrated books were copied. Illustrated herbals and books of medicinal ingredients (simples) seem to have fared better than most other sorts of medical illustration as survivors. Practical considerations undoubtedly played some part in ensuring that the essential means of recognising plants and other natural products were copied, but the largest group of these herbals, the ones associated with Pseudo-Apuleius, are in fact distinguished by the inclusion of far more non practical pictures than usual (see pp. 61-67). They contain any number of men fighting snakes and dogs, gods and goddesses, and scenes from mythology. Originally these were included to show how a plant had been used in a famous case-history or story, but the mistakes of later copyists show that they did not always know what these scenes meant. The copyists simply drew and painted what was in front of them, without any thought as to the practical value of such scenes.

In some cases, particularly in the fields of cautery and surgery, the copyists preserved illustrations which had become separated from their accompanying texts (Fig. 5); for instance, three operation scenes, probably deriving originally from south Italian manuscripts (Fig. 71-73), were copied in a monastery in the valley of the Meuse in the 12th century. Here the copyists definitely repeated visual details which they did not understand. Despite all the gaps and imperfections in the existing tradition of illustration, very few new elements seem to have been interpolated in the manuscripts by the monastic copyists themselves before the 13th century. The appearance of new secular illuminating workshops in the 13th century broke up the established pattern, introducing new subject matter for illustration.

How and why the lay scriptoria and illuminating shops came into being is not at all clear, for the records of their work in this early period – apart from the books themselves – have vanished almost without trace. But many of them must have taken their origin from the stationery and book trades necessary to the universities, whose rise in the 13th century is better documented. At Paris, Oxford, Bologna, and other studia, institutions for the rapid dissemination of texts were vital if students were not to spend all their time in laborious taking of dictation. The new mendicant orders of Franciscans and Dominicans, with their commitment to teaching, also created a demand for more and more portable texts. But all these things are not sufficient explanation for the development of lay illuminating shops. After all, the emphasis at the universities was on the copying and studying of texts, which had to be as cheap as possible, not the creation of elaborate and expensive miniatures. What is more, before the early 14th century only a handful of medical texts had actually entered the curriculum – chiefly the texts that made up the famous *articella* (see below, pp. 21-22) – and these are very seldom found illustrated.

A factor of greater significance, perhaps, in the rise of the lay illuminating shops was the stimulus given to fine book production by court patronage in France. During the reign of St Louis (1226 – 1270), France took a lead in the patronage of all the arts, including of course that of book-painting, which it was not to surrender for two centuries or more. The example of the court was followed by nobles and churchmen in Paris and the provinces, and imitated in other European countries. One major consequence of this growth in patronage was an expansion of secular manuscript production of all types. The beginnings of illustration of romances, histories, and chansons de geste, as well as works of science in different branches, can be traced to this period. This is the context in which illumination of new medical texts should be seen, rather than as a branch of book production in its own right. The sort of narrative illustration found in the *Chirurgia* ('Surgery') of Roger Frugardi (see pp. 84-86), with 'action scenes' of operations, some in a connected sequence, is best understood by analogy with the techniques of illustration employed in the romances, histories, and moralised bibles being turned out by the same workshop at the same time.

Language is important here too. French had become the fashionable language of Europe, so it is not surprising that French language texts, like the translation of Roger Frugardi's *Chirurgia*, were favourite objects for illumination. Practical manuals of health written originally in French, like that of Aldobrandino da Siena (see pp. 103-107), also required new programmes of illustration, if they were to satisfy the taste of the fashionable book-buyer. There was a new class of buyer for this sort of text, the layman who wished his book to be as expensively illuminated as he could afford, and to provide him with visual amusement and distraction.

So by the end of the 13th century the scope and nature of medical illustration had begun to change profoundly, and it is not surprising that so many of the older pictorial traditions maintained by the monastic copyists should have come to an end at this time. The monastic scriptoria from then on tended to

Fig. 6
Battlefield surgery. Hannibal and the Carthaginians lay siege to a city in this history of the Romans. Written and illuminated for Philip the Bold, Duke of Burgundy, in 1465.
Florence, Biblioteca Laurenziana, Med. Palat. 156, vol.1, f. 181v

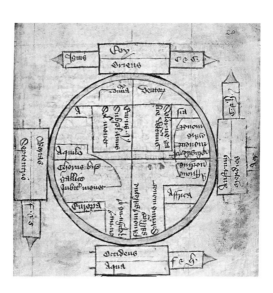

Fig. 7
Diagram of the winds, from a manuscript
of John of Arderne's surgical writings.
Asia is at the top (east) of this diagram,
Europe and Africa below.
As well as the winds, the diagram shows
the four elements and the four qualities.
BL, Sloane MS 795, f. 20

concentrate on religious themes, leaving the secular literary and scientific manuscripts to the lay illuminating shops.

SKETCHES AND DIAGRAMS

So far we have been talking about the making of highly finished illuminated manuscripts, requiring a considerable investment of time and resources, whether in monastic house or lay workshop. There were, however, less costly forms of illustration which went on throughout our period, little affected by the changes we have just been discussing. The sort of illustration that could be supplied by the scribe of a manuscript using only ink or crayon has its origins in the school-rooms of the Carolingian period. Isidore of Seville's *De natura rerum* ('On the nature of things') of c. 612 – 620 AD was the best known schoolbook from the 8th to the 10th century AD, used across most of Europe. It included a basic geographical diagram, the *rota terrarum*, dividing the world into three parts of a sphere – Asia, Europe, and Africa. There was also a circular scheme of the four elements (earth, air, fire, and water), and the qualities (hot, cold, moist, and dry), which was sometimes elaborated to include the four seasons, and the four humours (blood, phlegm, yellow bile, black bile).

In an environment where copies of texts were thin on the ground, these diagrams provided excellent visual aids, which the student could use to master basic concepts of natural philosophy. Greek natural philosophy, where it concerned elements, qualities, humours, ages, or seasons, lent itself very easily to visual display, because of its obsession with the number four. Concepts could be represented conveniently as divisions of squares, or orthogonal crosses within circles. So, long before the full complexities of the theories of Galen became known to the Latin West (see pp. 21-24), simple diagrams of the basic distinctions are to be found in manuscripts.

As full-blown Galenism took hold, from the 12th century onwards, more and more of these diagrams came to be needed in specif-

ically medical contexts. The microcosmic human body had to be shown linked in numerous ways with the fourfold divisions of the macrocosm (the elements, the seasons, etc.). For instance, two common types of diagram are often found in the treatises on practical medicine and surgery of John of Arderne, a 14th-century English writer best known for his work on *fistula-in-ano* (see pp. 89-91). One of these two diagrams integrates the winds, elements, qualities, and a compass rose; the second deals with the balance of the humours at different times of the day. Whereas the balance of the humours diagram illustrates a specific point in the text, the first and larger diagram was evidently intended to orientate the reader generally in regard to macrocosmic influences on man.

This larger diagram is shown in Fig. 7. Although the diagram looks very jumbled at first sight, the different components can be sorted out one from the other without too much difficulty. Within the circle lies an orthogonal cross, which intersects the circle at the four compass points (east is at the top, as is usual in medieval diagrams). Another layer of information is provided by a *mappa*

Fig. 8
Suturing a head wound. A marginal illustration
to 'the glosses of the four masters' (of Salerno),
from an early 14th-century manuscript
Wellcome MS 544, p. 22

mundi or *rota terrarum*, dividing the world into three continents - Asia, Europe, and Africa. Europe and African can be seen in the lowest segments of the circle, at the north-west and south-west of the compass rose respectively. Asia lies in a band across the upper eastern part of the circle. In the captions which make tangents to the circle at the four cardinal points are listed the elements which correspond to each of the points. Fire is east, air is south, water is west, and earth is north. In the same captions the combinations of qualities are also indicated: working from east clockwise – warm and dry, warm and wet, cold and wet, cold and dry. Finally we have the winds, each placed in their appropriate quarter from the centre of the compass rose. The names of the winds given include not only the four major winds at the cardinal points, Aeolus, Auster, Zephyr, and Boreas, but also the so-called 'ministerial' winds at south-east, south-west, etc. There are even indications of which winds are moved by which planets – Choros in the north-west sector is moved by Jupiter, according to the caption. This complicated interlocking of geographical, meteorological, astronomical and physical data shows how much the learned physician or surgeon of the 14th century had to integrate into his understanding of sickness and health.

Not all the ink sketches in medical manuscripts are schematic diagrams of this type. There are also anatomical sketches, marginal drawings of symptoms or procedures, pictures of instruments inserted within a line of text, and many other types. Fig. 8 is an example of the sort of sketch which occurs not as part of a deliberate programme of illustration, but as an expression of the fancy of the scribe. This drawing occurs in the bottom margin of a section in Wellcome MS 544 devoted to the so-called 'glosses of the four masters'. This text was supposed to have been written by four masters of the famous medical school of Salerno, towards the end of the 13th century. It consists of glosses to a well-known book on surgery of the mid 13th century, that of Roland of Parma. Our illustration is underneath chapters of the first book of the text dealing with wounds to the head. There are specific references in it to the pro-

cedure for suturing a head-wound, but our illustration would not be of much practical help to anyone wanting to learn the technique. The surgeon seems almost to be standing on the shoulders of the much larger patient, and wields an awesome needle. The spontaneity of this kind of sketch makes a striking contrast with the more tradition-bound work of the illuminator.

GALENISM

We have already seen that the interpretation of many diagrams in medieval manuscripts is impossible without reference to Galenic theories of medicine. It is time to attempt a brief sketch of these theories, for the whole of medieval medicine may be described as Galenic. Individual writers, especially amongst the Arabs, took issue with Galen over certain specific points, but every medical author of the Middle Ages worked within the framework of Galenic ideas. Galen (see Fig. 9) himself lived in the 2nd century AD, and of his voluminous writings on medicine and philosophy only fragments were known to the western Middle Ages, and these in translation. But these fragments carried more weight with medieval philosophers than any other medical writings, and were supplemented by western translations of Arabic authors – who themselves built their systems on what they knew of Galenic medicine. The fundamental tenets of Galenism were most familiar to westerners in the shape of the *articella*, where Galen and his Arabic commentators were found side-by-side. The *articella* was a group of texts which formed the staple of university teaching of medicine in Europe from the 12th century to the 16th century.

The components of the *articella* varied at different times and places, but most often it contained the *Isagoge* of Johannitius, the *Aphorisms* and *Prognostics* of Hippocrates, and short works on urine and pulse. Later the *Tegni* (or Ars parva, 'Short theory of medicine') of Galen was added, and also the *De regimine acutorum* ('Regimen in acute diseases') of Hippocrates, with a commentary by Galen. The name of Hippocrates is more to the fore here than that of Galen, but the Hippocratic writ-

Fig.9
Galen, depicted as one of the twelve 'masters of nature', one born in each month of the year, from a German manuscript of 1443/4. He is associated with February, and as with the others depicted in this manuscript, has a distinctly oriental appearance.
BL, Additional MS 15697, f. 33

Fig. 10
Rolando lectures from his book to students.
Rolando da Parma, *Chirurgia*, c.1300.
Rome, Biblioteca Casanatense, MS 1382, f. 3

ings were not valued as a distinct source of medical ideas. Galen himself had been willing to concede the prior authority of Hippocrates, and indeed praised him extravagantly, but Hippocrates came to the medieval West packaged by Galen, and often attended by Galen's own commentaries. Hippocrates's writings, or rather those ascribed to him, can to all intents and purposes be regarded as an integral part of Galenism.

Although the *articella* is found so often in manuscripts, it is not very often found illustrated. This is not because of intrinsic lack of illustrative interest so much as because texts copied for university use needed to be copied quickly and their costs kept down to a minimum. One *articella* text in the British Library is illustrated, however – with miniatures of the authors of the component texts in the form of historiated initials at the beginning of each. The text is written in a university bookhand of c.1300, and is extensively annotated with marginal and interlinear glosses. The glosses provided interpretations of theoretical terms, and explanations of difficult points.

One miniature depicts Hippocrates, at the beginning of the treatise *De regimine acutorum*, and it is shown here in Fig. 11. No portrait tradition for Hippocrates existed in the Middle Ages, so he is shown simply as a contemporary university doctor of medicine, with his long robe and cap. What mattered here, as in the case of most author portraits of the Middle Ages, was not resemblance, but the idea of authority. We may suppose that the patient in bed is suffering from one of the continuous fevers which Hippocrates says are the mark of acute sickness. Pleurisy, pneumonia, phrenitis, and 'ardent' fever all have their appropriate regimen. Hippocrates made little use of drugs and medicines, recommending different forms of diet, or purges, or letting blood instead. Hippocrates may here be administering liquid from a sponge or shallow dish, because much of the text concerns the virtues of hydromel, oxymel, wine, and, above all, ptisan (barley water). The presence of a third party at the bedside may indicate that this is a clinical scene with a student, or he may just be an attendant.

But of all the tracts which make up the *articella*, the *Ars parva* or *Tegni* of Galen takes us straight to the heart of Galenism. It offers a series of definitions which explain the scope of the theory and practice of medicine. Medicine is 'knowledge of what is healthy, morbid, and neutral'. The body is completely healthy when the four qualities (hot, cold, dry, moist) are in complete harmony, though one or other quality can prevail without necessarily leading to clinical illness. Only when the specific functions of the body are harmed is illness present. The organic parts (brain, liver, heart, etc.) are the instruments by which the body functions. Each of these principal parts, and the other parts which depend on them, as well as the body as a whole, have their own temperaments (that is, qualitative mixtures, in which one or other of the qualities predominates). The diagnostic description of these different temperaments takes up about one-third of the book and is the most typically Galenic part of medicine.

All substances, including food and drink, are said to be made up of the four elements (fire, air, earth, and water) which in the process of digestion are turned into the bodily juices, the humours, of which there are (once again) four kinds (blood, phlegm, yellow bile, and black bile). These humours nourish the tissues of the body, and lack or excess of them causes disease, just like changes in the qualities of the organic parts of the body.

All this makes it sound as if the body was balanced on a knife-edge of health, but in fact Galenism allowed considerable leeway between the ideal state of health on the one hand and illness on the other. This in turn encouraged lengthy consideration of relationships between the different temperaments of individuals, and the diet and ways of life which might affect them, in health as in sickness.

Our sketch of Galenism must necessarily be of the thumb-nail variety; it should not be forgotten that these concepts, with their endless permutations, gave the academic physician excellent opportunities to elaborate his diagnosis, to prepare detailed advice on regimen for his patient, and to prescribe compound medicines with long lists of ingredients. Further complexity was introduced (though not in this little tract) by the subsequent subdivision of each quality into four different degrees of intensity, so that diet and regimen could be put on a quantifiable basis.

ARABIC INFLUENCES

The *articella*, and fully-fledged Galenism in medieval medicine, were only the end-products of a period of translation and intellectual assimilation in the 11th and 12th centuries. Not only the Arab authors, like Johannitius, but Galen himself had first to be translated from Arabic. The fragments of medicine which had survived in Latin down to the 11th century could not in themselves provide sufficient materials for the theoretical outlook of Galenism. The title *Tegni* itself is only a Latin transliteration of the Arabic term for the *Ars parva* of Galen. In south Italy and in Moslem Spain an enormous exercise in translation of the medical works had to take place before the treasures of Galenic medicine could be unlocked for Western scholars. Some of the translators, like Constantine the African and Gerard of Cremona, were actually credited with authorship of some of these works which they had translated from the Arabic. The writings of the *articella* were among the first to be translated, which explains why these particular works, not in themselves the most important of the Galenic corpus, should have assumed such importance in the university curriculum. In the 13th and 14th centuries other more extensive and systematic works, principally the great medical encyclopaedias of the Arabs, the *Canon* of Avicenna, the *Continens* of Rhazes, the *Liber regius* of Haly Abbas, and the *Colliget* of Averroes, were also translated. A scholastic industry grew up around Galenism, as it had around Aristotelianism .

It would be a mistake to think of the Arab authors as mere conduits for classical medicine to the West. In attempting to synthesise the heritage of Greek medicine bequeathed to them by their own great era of translation, in the 9th century AD, they re-interpreted some specific concepts, and

Fig. 11
Hippocrates medicating a patient.
The bed-ridden patient is probably suffering
from a fever, and Hippocrates seems
to be administering a liquid from a sponge
or shallow dish. No tradition of Hippocratic
portraiture survived into the 13th century,
when this miniature was made,
so Hippocrates is shown as a contemporary
university physician.
BL, Harley MS 3140, f. 39

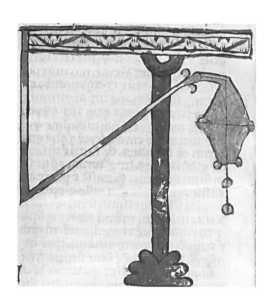

Fig. 12
A vaginal speculum. The screw at the bottom is
supposed to open and close two blades at the top,
but the artist has missed the mechanical point
altogether. The curious kite shape
on the right should be a separate scalpel.
From a 14th-century Latin manuscript of Albucasis.
BL, Additional MS 36617, f. 28v

systematised what in Galen's own writings
had sometimes been left vague or in a state
of self-contradiction. Although they worked
very much within the framework of Galenic
philosophy, they were not afraid to contra-
dict the master on points of empirical detail.
In fact the greatest Arab authors were considerable clinicians, who were able to sup-
plement theoretical statements with a wealth
of observations based on clinical experience.
On the other hand, they did not bother to
systematise the more speculative and philosophical parts of Galen's writings – this was
a tendency which became stronger as the
Arab authors themselves were translated into
Latin. The Arabs had seized on Galen to fill
the gap in their philosophical outlook made
by the lack of a strong tradition in natural
philosophy and medicine, when compared
to their own highly developed disciplines of
history, poetry, rhetoric and law. So there
was a great deal in Galenism which was in
fact of Arab origin, and a fair portion of
Galen himself left out.

ISLAM AND MEDICAL ILLUSTRATION

The extent to which the Arab authors were
hostile to illustration, especially when it represented the human form, has been much
exaggerated. It would be perfectly possible to
compile a book which drew entirely on Islamic medical manuscripts for its illustrations.
The theme of the Islamic contribution to
medical illustration is too large to be tackled
within the confines of this book. But because,
in a few areas, it exerted such a powerful influence on Western illustration, something must
be said about it here. One such area is the
depiction of surgical instruments. A set of as
many as 200 instruments are found very frequently in Arabic texts of Albucasis (to give
him the name he was known by in the West).
Albucasis, who lived in Spain, and died in
1013, wrote a large encyclopaedia of surgery,
which devoted its thirtieth book to surgical
instruments. Many of the instruments
described by Albucasis, and illustrated most
clearly in the Arabic manuscripts, were invented by the Arabs themselves, rather than copied
from classical models.

In the 12th century, Albucasis was translated into Latin by Gerard of Cremona. Latin
translations of Albucasis tended to follow the
Arabic text word for word, and the drawings
of instruments seem to have been copied in
the same spirit. Even the mistakes made by
Arabic copyists were simply repeated by their
Western counterparts. Fig. 12 shows a vaginal speculum on similar lines to instruments
known to have been used in Roman medicine, as well as in Islam. This 14th-century
picture is a faithful copy of an Arabic design
in a manuscript now in the Bodleian Library
in Oxford. It is so faithful that it reproduces
the curious hanging feature on the right-hand
side of the illustration. In the Arabic manuscript a faint caption tells us that this feature
ought to be a separate picture of a double
edged scalpel. It is clear that the Western artist
did not understand the mechanical princi-
ples of the instrument he copied. For a start,
it is upside-down, and the decorated bar at
the top of our picture should consist of two
separate blades. These blades were meant to
be opened and shut by means of a screw,
which is the six-lobed shape at the foot of the
illustration. These are not designs which could
ever have been used as blueprints for surgical instrument making in the West.

The example shows only too clearly the
likelihood of a manuscript tradition of illustration becoming corrupt through the process
of copying. But it also shows the indebted-
ness of Western manuscript illustration to the
Arabic tradition, just as in the case of the texts
of Galenic medicine.

MAGICAL AND RELIGIOUS DEFENCES AGAINST ILLNESS

Galenism, whether in Arab dress, or in its
naturalised Western forms, was pre-eminently
an intellectual approach to medicine. It could
be accommodated within the scholastic framework of teaching at the universities. But, of
course, there were other less intellectual forms
of healing practised in the Middle Ages. The
empirical and semi-magical means of healing employed by the illiterate do not generally leave much trace in books, however successful in practice, though they may play a

very important role in the oral culture of a predominantly rural society. So far as illustration is concerned, then, this dimension of healing remains unrepresented. We do however occasionally find charms written out in medical books, particularly in antidotaries or herbals. We must assume that they were employed alongside more rational methods on the principle that if both rational and magical means are available, it is as well to try both.

Another weapon in the fight against sickness was the practice of praying to particular saints who were supposed to have healing powers. Members of the body or diseases were often associated with one particular saint. Thus St Apollonia was the patroness of dentistry; St Benignus was the patron saint of sufferers with chilblains. This invocation of saints found occasional visual expression, because many private books of devotion contained prayers to, and images of, favourite healing saints.

One fine example from a book of hours illustrated for François de Dinteville, Bishop of Auxerre, in 1525, is shown in Fig. 13. It is a picture of St Roch, who was supposed to protect his devotees against the plague. St Roch was born in Montpellier, and died there in 1327; a cult grew up in the south of France as a result of these local connections. It was natural therefore for the Bishop of Auxerre to have a miniature of Roch included in his personal book of hours. The miniature shows Roch in the garb of a pilgrim to Rome, standing in a rocky wilderness. On his way to Rome, having already healed many plague sufferers by prayer and by touch, Roch had himself caught plague in Piacenza. He went out of the city to avoid infecting others, and found a refuge in neighbouring woods. Legend relates that St Roch was tended by a little dog that foraged for food on his behalf, and by an angel who came down from heaven to dress his sores. All these parts of the story are reflected in the picture.

Saints like Sebastian and Roch, who were supposed to heal those afflicted with plague, were objects of peculiar veneration, the more so since rational medicine seemed to have so

little to offer in the face of plague. But when the plague had passed, invocation of spiritual powers for healing purposes did not stop. It was a perpetual refrain in the prayers and devotions of ordinary men and women. Much of medieval religious life was coloured by the belief that the healing power attributed to Christ, and passed on at Pentecost, was literally as well as figuratively effective. A whole range of practices, such as pilgrimage of the sick, writing of holy names on scrolls worn on the body, *ex voto* offerings of models of

Fig. 13
St Roch, depicted in a wilderness outside Piacenza, where he caught the plague on a pilgrimage to Rome. His sores are attended to by an angel, while a dog brings him his food.
From a French book of hours, 1525.
BL, Additional MS 18854, f. 146v

limbs and organs, can only be explained by belief in the healing virtues of faith. Of the thousands of miracle stories current in the period, the most important single category was that of the healing of the hopelessly ill (see Fig. 14). These things had nothing directly to do with medical books or pictures, but they should not be forgotten as a dimension of healing in the Middle Ages.

USERS AND PRACTITIONERS

For whose use were manuscripts containing medical illustrations made? What part did they play in the pattern of medical practice, as opposed to the transmission of knowledge? These are important questions, but very difficult to answer, because so often the manuscripts themselves tell us nothing about their owners except their names, and very little about the ways in which they were used. Those owners who have left their names in the manuscripts are for the most part unknown to history, and reveal nothing about their rank or occupation. In the earlier Middle Ages we can sometimes connect a manuscript with a particular monastery: we know for instance that Sloane MS 1975 (see Figs. 57, 72, 73) was owned by the monastery of Ourscamp, a Cistercian house near Noyon, north of Paris. We may deduce that a monastery which could commission, or have written within its walls, such a luxurious item, possessed a library, and may have been active in the production of fine books. But what we still do not know is whether the monks would have used the highly formalised plant depictions to identify medicinal simples, and whether the sort of surgery illustrated in the same manuscript was ever actually practised within the infirmary of Ourscamp.

In the case of other early manuscripts which we may assume were in the possession of monastic houses (though without knowing necessarily which they were), there is sometimes evidence in the form of recipes added in later hands, or other sorts of gloss. These tell us that the manuscript was used by someone with a practical interest in medicine. This is the case with Cotton MS Vitellius C III, an Anglo-Saxon herbal (see Fig.3), which con-

tains not only glosses from the 11th and 12th centuries, but additional information added as late as the 17th century (by William Harvey, discoverer of the circulation of the blood, no less). A 14th-century catalogue by Prior Eastry of Christ Church, Canterbury, indicates that the manuscript may well have been owned by the monastery there. We know that monasteries had infirmaries for their inmates and sometimes for outsiders too; we know that they had flourishing herb gardens and took an active interest in the spice trade with the East. So when there is evidence of glossing we can probably assume that a manuscript was consulted for medicinal purposes.

When it comes to private ownership, the situation is altogether murkier. Only in the case of one of the medical manuscripts illustrated in this book is it possible to name an owner, and then say something about who he was, what he did, and the use to which he put his book. He was Richard Ferris, Master of the Barber-Surgeons Company of London, Sergeant-Surgeon to Queen Elizabeth I, and he inscribed his name in Sloane MS 2463 (see pp. 39-40). This early 16th-century manuscript contains texts in Latin and English on anatomy and surgery, as well as an antidotary, and a section on gynaecology. This last is illustrated by drawings of the positions of the foetus in the womb. Ferris, though not a university-trained physician, obviously does not fit the stereotype of the 16th-century sawbones, unlettered and untrained (a stereotype fostered by the university-trained physicians themselves). Many prominent surgeons were equally as learned as their physician counterparts.

The 16th-century hand which has glossed the manuscript throughout may well be that of Ferris himself. Though at some time in the 16th century a price of 48s 4d was put upon the book, a considerable sum for those days, it is likely that Ferris did not just acquire this book as a bibliophile, but meant to use it. Not only the glossing, but the fact that all the texts fit together as a guide to general surgery, support this conclusion. Still it is hard to imagine that these illustrations of foetal positions would have been of much help to Ferris if he had been called upon to supervise the delivery of the Queen's baby!

Ferris was not typical of the owners of this sort of book, in that he was a professional medical practitioner, and achieved high status. Before the first appearance of medical texts in the vernacular (in England – excluding Anglo-Saxon texts – this meant in Anglo-Norman in the 13th century, though it was earlier in other European countries), we can assume that only those who had received a Latin education would have commissioned or bought medical books. Many, if not most, must have been clerics (although not always in the case of the *de luxe* items). The secular clergy could, and did, pursue a medical qualification and enter into practice as licensed physicians. So if anyone could be regarded as the typical reader of medical texts outside the monastic houses in the early Middle Ages, it must be the learned clerk. The decree of the Fourth Lateran Council in 1215 forbade those in major orders – deacons, subdeacons, and priests – that part of surgery which involved burning and cutting, but it made little difference to the clerical practice of medicine in general. Operative surgery was too small a part of medicine, and clerks in major orders were too small a proportion of the total.

With the coming of the vernaculars as learned languages, the situation changed, since anyone literate – women, bailiffs and other officials on landed estates, or tradespeople, for example – could now have access to medical literature. What they had access to, however, was still based firmly on the translation of the Latin university texts. It was not a new species of literature based on the experience of the humble country leech or 'wise-woman'. But in the course of the flurry of translating activity that was involved in order to open up the university medical literature to new classes of practitioner, a final winnowing out of the more theoretical elements took place. The emphasis in the vernacular texts is very much on diagnosis and prognosis, prevention and treatment of disease, rather than on anatomy, the causes of disease, or the refinement of humoral theory. Of course, the vernacular translators were only pushing to its furthest limits a process that began with compilers of medical compendia in the centuries after Galen's death.

Fig. 14
Praying to St Paul
for delivery from
sickness. From
a 15th-century
manuscript
of Paul's Letters.
Florence,
Biblioteca Laurenziana,
MS Plut. 23.6, f. 128

Fig. 15
Dame Trotula. She is holding an orb in her left hand,
signifying that she is an 'empress' among midwives
Wellcome MS 544, p. 65

The commissioner or purchaser of this sort of literature was increasingly likely in the 14th and 15th centuries to be drawn from outside the charmed circle of university-trained physicians and clerics. At Oxford and Cambridge medicine established itself as an academic discipline on the model of the Italian or French *studia*, but the number of physicians trained there in the 14th and 15th centuries was very small. Yet this does not seem to have had an inhibiting effect on the number of English medical manuscripts produced. In fact, to judge from the enormous growth in the number of manuscripts produced in the 15th century in particular, it seems certain that for the first time householders of relatively modest standing, but with a determination to gain practical advice on health matters, were acquir-

ing medical books for their own use. There may even have been workshops in London which specialised in producing medical books; this is suggested by the standardisation of script and layout within groups of such manuscripts. There were many willing and able to obtain books from which to make copies in their own hand, too – although this is less common than might be assumed, the materials and skills necessary for the making of manuscripts not being readily available to all and sundry.

WOMEN

Women make their first appearance as acquirers and annotators of English manuscripts in the 15th century. Even well-born ladies did not feel it below their dignity to diagnose and prescribe for ailments within the household. In medical illustration, however, women of all classes appear far more often as patients than as medical practitioners. A well-dressed lady does appear in the cupping scenes from one 15th-century manuscript (see Fig. 89); but even there she is seen in the role of an ancillary, for cupping was one of the manual parts of medical practice, and regarded therefore as less prestigious. The pictures must give a misleading idea of the scale of the activities of women, as well as of their importance. In rural communities 'wise women' and midwives no doubt did much of the prescribing and treatment required, without the help of books. But there were women who achieved the status of recognised practitioners, with a proper knowledge of the medical authorities, particularly in Italy. Still more women practised strictly within the circle of their family or household, where books in the vernacular could play a vital role in passing down a modicum of medical knowledge from generation to generation.

In the kingdom of Naples women were allowed to practise surgery and gynaecology after they had passed an examination by royal physicians and surgeons. This was simply official recognition of the fact that women had always been expected to take a leading role in obstetrics and minor surgery – an expectation that surely accounts for the eager-

ness of later copyists to attribute to a certain Dame Trotula, or Dame Trot, of Salerno, authorship of the best-known passages on obstetrics in the Middle Ages. We cannot be certain who the author was, or even that these passages were the work of a woman. But in one Wellcome manuscript, the text known as 'Trotula minor', which may well date from Salerno in the 12th century, is actually headed by a picture of the legendary Trotula, carrying an orb (see Fig. 15). Her status here has become that of 'Queen of Midwives', and we can easily imagine the practising midwife invoking the help of such a figure.

STRUCTURE OF THE BOOK

The remaining five chapters of this book divide the province of medicine up into broad areas, signified by the chapter headings. These are no hard and fast boundaries; some of the illustrations might equally as well have appeared under one heading as another. All such divisions are of course artificial, and tend to impose anachronistic modern ideas on the medieval medical book and its illustration. Galenic medicine claimed to make one whole of all the different parts of medical theory and practice, which makes it all the more artificial to treat each part separately. Nevertheless some guiding ideas have to be used to approach the subject, and these divisions seem as good as any.

An attempt has been made to compensate for this artificiality by taking care not to twist the interpretation of any particular illustration to fit in with the theme of the chapter in which it occurs. Most illustrations will get separate discussion within the chapter to which they belong, and there are cross references from the text to the illustration in each case.

ANATOMY

At one end of the Library of the Wellcome Institute for the History of Medicine in London there used to stand a tall screen displaying enlargements of six imposing figures standing before a panoramic view of an Italian landscape. Each of these figures is flayed to reveal layer after layer of the muscles beneath the skin. They come from *De humani corporis fabrica* ('On the structure of the human body') by Andreas Vesalius, published in 1543 at Basel by Joannes Oporinus. It is the most important anatomical textbook ever published, and Vesalius not only wrote the text, but must have given detailed instructions to his draughtsman, who came from Titian's studio in Venice. Vesalius keyed the pictures to captions alongside, but also to the text itself, so that text and illustrations throw light on one another. He intended that the book should teach students of surgery sufficient anatomy to perform their own dissections, and practise their manual craft of healing with a better understanding of the structures of the human body.

But these figures posing dramatically against the Paduan landscape (see Fig. 16) are also masterpieces of graphic art in their own right, which could be reproduced in hundreds of identical copies. The skills of the wood-cutter and the master-printer were just as vital to this project as those of the designer and draughtsman. Vesalius's achievement was to bring together in one work the techniques of anatomy, art, and the printed book. The tableau in the Wellcome Library celebrated this achievement with the help of a technique unknown to Vesalius and his contemporaries – that of photography. So two revolutions in the history of illustration were commemorated in one series of pictures. When looking at the anatomical illustrations of the Middle Ages we have to think ourselves back into a world where neither of these revolutions had taken place. By comparison with the majestic designs of the *De fabrica*, the manuscript illustrations of the Middle Ages look crude and childish. But the illustrator of a manuscript did not share the same aims as Vesalius, and we should not judge him by the same standards. Not only was his anatomical knowledge weaker, but he did not have the technical resources for reproducing detailed images

Fig. 16
Woodcut of a muscle man, from Andreas Vesalius, *De humani corporis fabrica* (Basel, 1543).

again and again. Each manuscript meant a single unique text, and a single unique picture. Because the copying of images from manuscript to manuscript was just as vulnerable to mistakes and omissions as the copying of texts, there was every reason to try to keep them simple. In any case, manuscript illustrations did not serve the same purpose as printed books. They were used most often to prompt the memory, by allowing the reader to remind himself at a glance of the function of different organs and members of the body. Pictures of structures needed to be clear, and not confused and overcrowded with detail. So what we see most often in medieval manuscripts are outline drawings, accompanied usually by short texts and captions which, for example, remind the reader of the places to let blood, the seats of different diseases in the body, or the functions of the various organs and members. Since such essentially practical matters do not lend themselves to the art of the illuminator, we will not find many elaborately painted miniatures.

Although no anatomy illustrations survive from the classical world, we can judge from the surgical pictures in a Byzantine manuscript (Fig. 17) of the 11th century that a tradition of naturalistic images of the human form survived, at least in the East. Despite the stiffness and lack of proportion in these figures, they contrast sharply with surgical illustrations from the medieval West (Fig. 18), which treat the human figure in a much more schematic fashion. Nevertheless there is a lot to be learnt from these comparatively crude and schematic figures about the medicine of the period, and about attitudes to the human form. What they lack in polish, they make up for in vigour, and they are packed with interesting and entertaining detail. Each one has its own individual charm, because designed and executed by one man. But the designs are not spontaneous inspirations of the artist. In most cases he was copying another manuscript; and the designs used are remarkably consistent. So far as full-length figures are concerned, or the internal organs of the body, time and again we are led back to one basic series. This was christened the 'five picture series' by Karl Sudhoff, a great German historian of medicine, who catalogued and photographed dozens of manuscripts which contained the series, early in this century.

Sudhoff described a series of five figures, depicting the veins, arteries, bones, nerves, and muscles of the human body. In the first examples these systems were shown within an outline figure drawn in a squatting position, with the arms pointing downwards. Sudhoff thought the original series, of which the earliest known example dates from the 12th century, might go as far back as the great anatomy school of Alexandria in the 2nd century AD. Lately it has been suggested that they descend instead from Arabic authors who systematised the anatomical works of Galen, and that they may have reached West-

Fig. 17
The naked figures of physician and patient represent the survival of classical ideals in this Byzantine manuscript of the commentary of Apollonius of Citium on the *De articulis* of Hippocrates, 11th century. *Florence, Biblioteca Laurenziana, MS Plut. 74.7, f. 195v*

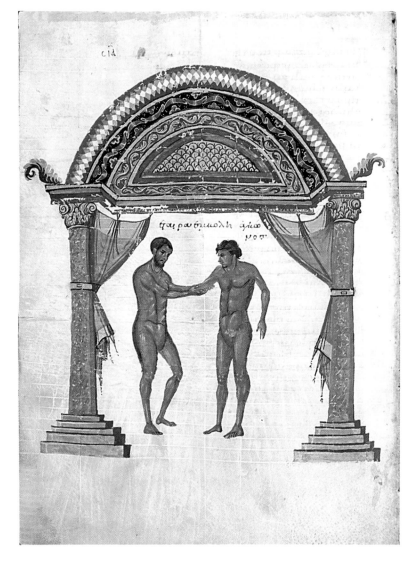

ern Europe in the 11th or 12th centuries, via England. Whatever their origin, they are a vital medieval link between ancient schemes of the body, and post-Vesalian illustrators, who still draw schemes of the different physiological systems in today's textbooks.

Recently it has become apparent that there are more than five pictures in this series. The text which goes with them in the famous Apocalypse manuscript at the Wellcome Library states that the author will treat in his *Figura incisionis* (literally 'figure of cutting') of nine systems in all – (1) arteries, (2) veins, (3) bones, (4) nerves, (5) muscles, (6) genitalia, (7) stomach, liver and viscera, (8) matrix (womb), (9) brain and eyes. In fact pictures of eight of this series (all except that of the brain and eyes) can be identified in the Wellcome manuscript. As we shall see, figures of the brain and eyes are quite frequently met with in medieval anatomical illustration, though usually on their own, or in connection with treatises about the eye. By the 15th century, when the Wellcome manuscript was written, the squatting figure has given way to a standing pose, and items (6)-(9) are not framed by a human figure at all.

The anatomical and medical drawings in the Wellcome Apocalypse are only a part of a larger series of 292 emblematic and symbolic drawings which turn this religious encyclopaedia into a picture-book. The manuscript seems to have been written and illustrated about 1420, and several of the texts are in a Middle German dialect. However our *Figura incisionis* drawings are accompanied by a Latin text, purporting to be by Galen himself. Though the anatomical drawings have tinted outlines, like the religious ones, and the same range of pale colours are employed, they are not by the same artist or artists.

One of the series is shown in Fig. 19 – the muscle man. The squatting posture of earlier manuscripts here gives way to a much more natural upright stance, and he seems to stand on a grassy tussock, with one leg bent at the knee. He wears a small g-string, presumably for the sake of decency, though another of the anatomical pictures in this series does

Fig. 18
Cautery scenes. The patient's nakedness is often covered by underpants. Little effort is made to achieve anatomical likeness.

From Rolando da Parma, *Chirurgia*, c.1300. *Rome, Biblioteca Casanatense, MS 1382, f. 2v*

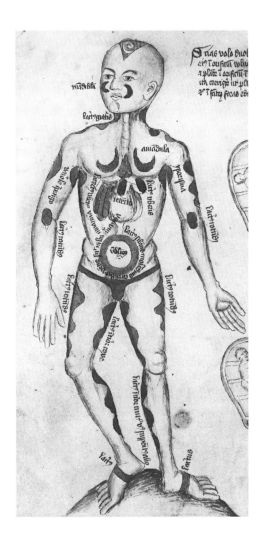

show the male genitals. The muscles themselves, captioned on and around the body, are shown in the traditional form of blobs or patches, rather arbitrary in shape. The names given to the muscles are not particularly informative either – mandible (cheek) and throat muscle, etc. Two on the chest labelled amindula seem to derive from Western transliteration of the Arabic word for almond, used by Arab medical authors to describe the tonsil. Either these muscles have migrated from their original position or the almond describes only the shape of the muscle. Whichever it is, there is a strong hint here of an Arabic model for the text and drawing.

The text for the muscle man tells us that muscle is a substance found in the body which is neither bone nor flesh, which fills cavities and joins one member to another. Muscles function as the mechanism by which the human will puts the body in motion. The mandible muscle controls the movement of the lips, for example, the throat muscle enables us to swallow, and the circular muscle in the abdomen allows the digestion and egestion of food from the stomach. This figure and text would not be of much help to the student who tried to interpret the structures he found in a dissection, but it would enable him to account for basic human functions like the movement of limbs or digestion. So it did not matter very much whether the muscles were accurately drawn, or even drawn in the right place. (It is a measure of its 'accuracy' that the scribe who captioned the figure has even absent-mindedly placed pox and impetigo on the man's right upper arm, as if he were a disease man rather than a muscle man.)

The diagram of the stomach (Fig. 20) also comes from the series of the *Figura incisionis* in the Wellcome manuscript. In Galenic medicine, the stomach is the place where food is assimilated, and 'cooked' by the natural heat of the body. It plays a vital role in transforming the elements present in food and drink into the humours of the body, and it is this function, rather than its anatomical structure, which shows up here. Food enters at the top of the stomach, and chyle produced as a result of coction (cooking), together with waste products, exits at the bottom. At diametri-

cally opposite points on the inner wall of the circular stomach are the four humours. At the top is phlegm, coloured green; at the bottom blood, coloured red; at the right is black bile, coloured black, and at the left yellow bile, coloured orange. The presence of the four humours does not signify that they have an anatomical home in the stomach, but that proper 'cooking' of food in the stomach is essential to maintain the balance between the four humours, which in turn keeps the body healthy. It is what the stomach does, not what its anatomical structure is, that matters here.

The stomach occurs again in another of the drawings of intestinal organs (Fig. 21), at the top left, enclosed by the five-lobed liver. Here its sac-like shape represents an attempt at rough anatomical outline, but the red 'eye' which appears in the middle is the gall-bladder, which should be in front of the liver (as it is in other manuscripts). In the bottom right drawing – again of the liver – the gall bladder with its two bile ducts is shown in correct position in front of the liver. Returning to the stomach and liver at the top left, the oesophagus or gullet, and the duodenum, which lead out of the stomach at opposite ends, seem to lead from the liver instead. The depiction of a liver with five lobes stems not from observation, of course, but from the description given in anatomical writings by Galen. There are two other small oval organs shown in this group, the lower of which is certainly the gall-bladder again, its central portion identified as the source of bile. What the other one is, coloured green and called mappa, we cannot be sure, though it may represent the greater omentum (a fold of the membrane which lines the abdomen and encloses the stomach, liver, spleen, etc.). No picture of the spleen seems to occur in this group, and the mappa is the wrong shape. Lastly we have another highly schematic drawing, in which an arrow head penetrates a diamond shape from the top. From the caption, but only from the caption, we can work out that this is meant to be a picture of the lungs, presumably with the trachea and carotid artery entering from the top. This particular drawing gives us no idea even of the function of the organ shown, though the caption does refer us to the common description of the lungs as 'feathered'.

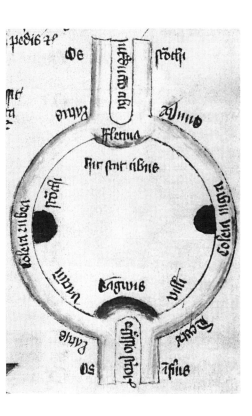

Fig. 20
The stomach. Food enters at the top, and is 'cooked' by natural heat in the stomach, while chyle and waste products exit at the bottom. The four humours are represented on the inner wall of the stomach. From the Wellcome Apocalypse, 15th century. *Wellcome MS 49, f. 36v*

In addition to the nine figures of the *Figura incisionis* series, the Wellcome manuscript contains several others not of that family, but often found in close proximity to it. Among these are some which belong to what we might call the alternative pathological series. Instead of the normal functioning of the healthy body, we have the wound man (see Fig. 84), the disease man and the disease woman. The disease figures are commonly shown in outline, just like the normal ones, but with names of diseases specific to various parts of the body written on, or captioned alongside, the figure. The largest and most striking of the pathological series in the Wellcome manuscript is the disease woman (Fig. 22). This figure is closer to the crouching figures of the earliest known anatomical drawings than the muscle man, although the contemporary head dress gives her a more realistic and modern appear-

ance. The names of organs and diseases are written over the body and all around her, and in the margins we also find suggested cures.

Female anatomy seems to differ little from the male, so far as internal organs are concerned, with the noteworthy exception that high on the left side of the woman's grossly distended stomach lies an inverted flask shape labelled *embrio*. The womb is shown impossibly distant from the cervix, while the intestines push the kidneys (with their lobes pointing the wrong way) to the opposite ends of the abdominal cavity. The real purpose of the illustration was evidently the listing and localising of the different diseases. There are not many diseases which could be said to be specifically female, save for an obvious few – the 'closed' womb, for instance. The diseases run from the usual afflictions of the head and face, (mania, running eyes, foul breath, etc.), written directly over the woman's head, to swelling feet, at the bottom of the picture. Amongst the recipes offered at the side is one for stimulating the flow of menstrual blood, involving herbs and animal substances decocted in wine. Putting together figure, captions, and the short text that goes with them, we have a package which would serve as a brief guide to any physician who had to deal with the illnesses of women, the emphasis being very much on practice rather than theory.

The disease woman of the Wellcome manuscript shows clearly how the draughtsmen of this sort of diagram used it to pack in all kinds of information about diagnosis and therapy, as well as anatomy. The human figure is used simply as a peg to hang it all on. This is a long way from the modern idea of an anatomical atlas, which treats a cross-section of the body in the spirit of a map. But, if we forget this modern idea for a moment, we can see that the medieval artists showed a sophisticated grasp of the techniques which we employ in modern diagrams – of the working parts of a machine for instance. If they did not invent the indication line, which points to a part of the whole figure, they certainly mastered its use. Sometimes the pointer is held by a disembodied hand. The same applies to the lines which divide a

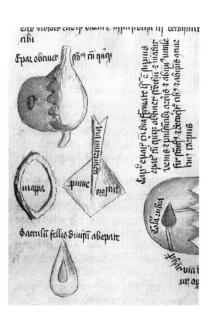

Fig. 21
Internal organs. At the top are the liver and stomach; below, the *mappa* (?), and the lungs (trachea and carotid artery enter at the top); and at the bottom, the gall bladder. On the right is the liver again, with the gall bladder in front of it. From the Wellcome Apocalypse. 15th century. *Wellcome MS 49, f. 36v*

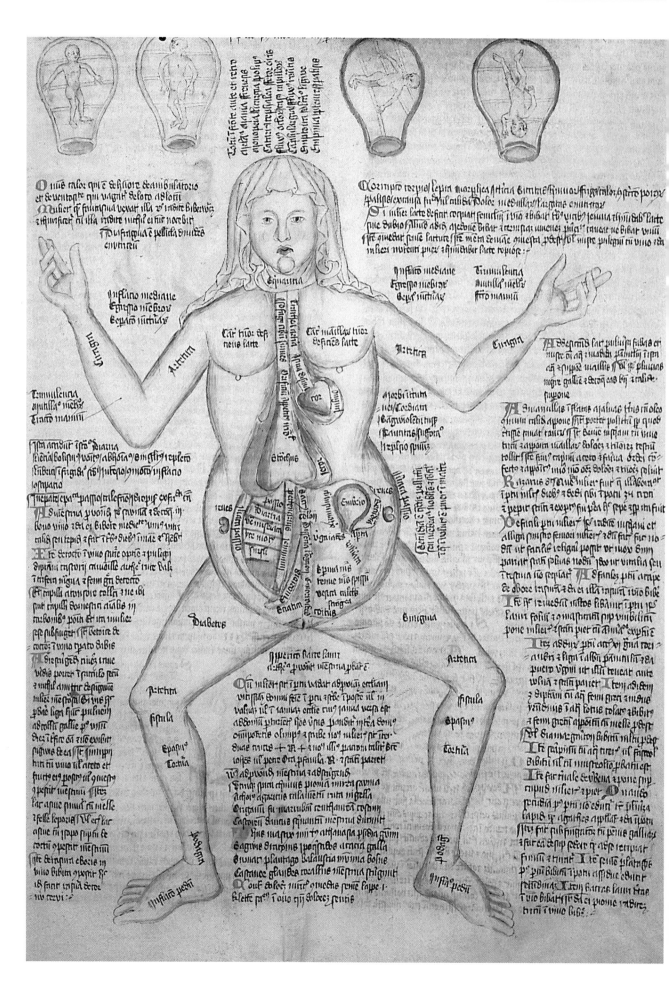

continuous area within an outline figure into separate compartments.

Good examples of both techniques can be found in a disease man from another 15th-century German manuscript (Fig. 23). This figure is the last of a sequence of diagrams running over three pages, which includes circular astronomical, geographical, and meteorological figures, and a blood-letting man (see pp. 95-97). The peculiar dancing pose of this man seems to have been a whim of the artist. It may have helped to maintain decency, though no such scruples are apparent in the blood-letting man. In any case this eccentricity does not stop the artist getting his information across. The lines running down to the skull divide the head up into compartments, each of which stands for the seat of one of the faculties of the mind. This leaves the skull itself free for the names of the bones of which it is made. A single indication line running from the base of the skull shows that the rear part of the brain is specified as the source of all the veins in the body. The cephalic, median, and hepatic veins are indicated by captions above the elbow on the right arm, at the spot usually favoured for blood-letting (there is a blood letting text on the other side of this leaf). Diseases are simply written over the general area affected. Sometimes the description is no more specific than the indication of place. The Latin term *cordia*, for instance, is written over the left breast, with the explanation that the German term is 'heart disease'. One of the more specific is *stranguinaria*, written in front of the man's abdomen – it means the inability to pass urine. This labelling technique is drafted into service yet again to indicate regions of the body which have a particular complexion (a blend of the qualities of heat and cold, dryness and moisture); the *tybia*, for example, placed here at the knee, is marked hot and dry. These anatomical figures were used as handy reference points at which significant medical information of all kinds could be conveniently grouped for quick retrieval.

The *Figura incisionis* series, and its pathological equivalent, do not exhaust the complement of figure illustrations of anatomy for the Middle Ages. As we might expect, there

are plenty of other skeletons to set alongside the bone man of the *Figura incisionis*. In the later Middle Ages, in the wake of the Black Death of 1348-50 there was a considerable vogue for the macabre in illuminations and in less exalted drawings. Scenes like the 'Dance of Death' allowed the illustrator to show skeletons performing like living men – though these sort of illustrations were generally poorly observed, because correct anatomy was not the point. But there are also skeletons which occur in strictly medical manuscripts, some of which have captions and labels to identify individual bones.

The most singular and accurate picture of the complete skeleton found in manuscript before the mid-16th century, however, may well be an uncaptioned and unaccompanied figure at the start of another German manuscript in the collections of the British Library (Fig. 24).

This manuscript is unusually well documented by the standards of most manuscripts of the period, since we know both the scribe and the date it was written. The scribe was one Contzen von Auerach, who finished his work on the Saturday after St Lucy's Day (i.e.

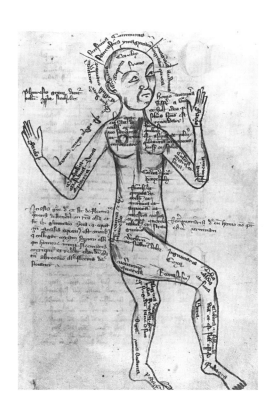

Fig 23
A disease man. This dancing figure is captioned with the names of different diseases to which the parts of the body are liable. There are also indications of the names of some bones, and of veins for letting blood in the arm. From a German 15th-century manuscript. *BL, Arundel MS 251, f. 37*

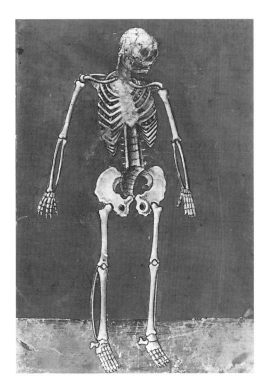

Fig. 24
Frontispiece to a German translation of the *Chirurgia Magna* of Bruno da Longoburgo, 1452. One of the most realistic pictures of a skeleton in the Middle Ages, despite some distortions and major omissions. *BL, Additional MS 21618, f. 1v*

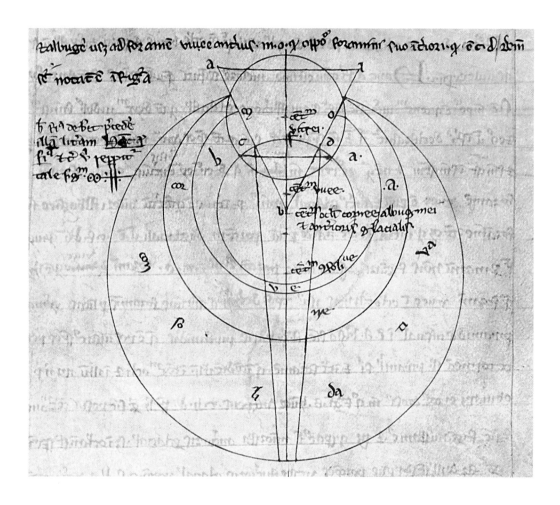

and partly by attempting to remain faithful to the actual appearance of the bones rather than merely suggesting their general relation to one another.

The anatomical detail of the skeleton is better than any to be found before the 16th century. Unusually, a real effort has been made to suggest the sutures or cracks in the top of the skull, even if the result is not entirely accurate. There is a curious extension of the temporal bone at the side of the head right down to the *processus transversus* of the atlas (the first cervical vertebra of the neck). The shoulder girdle is much more clearly and fully articulated than elsewhere Another positive feature is the picture of the lumbar vertebrae beneath the rib cage. Despite the unnaturally broad sternum, the rib-cage itself is not bad either; the joint between the cartilage and the rib proper is pointed up by an exaggerated kink. The artist does tend to muddle over the way that the lower or false ribs connect with the cartilage of the seventh rib above. The pelvic area is not so well done (as always in medieval skeletons), and the extremities of the body are also rather misleading (see the strange *os calcis* sticking out from the foot). But this is one of the few medical pictures from the Middle Ages where the artist gives every sign of having attempted to articulate the human skeleton in a pure spirit of observation. This may explain why the usual apparatus of captions and accompanying texts is missing.

Up to now we have concentrated on the full figure and internal organs of the body; but medieval anatomy did not stop there. One form of illustration grew directly out of geometry rather than medicine – diagrams of the structure of the eye. The earliest of these appears to date from the 13th century, and the stimulus was provided by the revival of mathematical theories of perspective under the influence of translations from the Arabic. Roger Bacon at Oxford was a prime mover in this field, and in a manuscript of his works from the 13th century come a number of geometrical figures meant to show how rays from external objects strike the crystalline humour in the centre of the eyeball (like all ancient and medieval philosophers he thought the

Fig. 25
A geometrical diagram of the eye, from a late 13th-century manuscript of the works of Roger Bacon. The diagram shows rays from outside entering the eye (at the top), and being refracted when they strike the crystalline humour at the centre of the eye.
BL, Royal MS 7 F VIII, f. 54v

14 December) 1465. The main work in the manuscript is the *Chirurgia Magna* ('Great Surgery') of Bruno da Longoburgo, in a German translation apparently made by one 'Meyster Prunus' in Pavia in Italy in 1452. The illustration of the skeleton was not necessarily meant to form a part of the surgery text; it simply happens to face the table of contents, and was obviously thought to be an appropriate frontispiece to the book.

Unfortunately the picture has been slightly rubbed, but it is still possible to appreciate how the artist succeeded by the use of shading with pen on parchment in making the detail of the bones stand out against the coloured background. The background is very simple – a light green base, indicating the earth, and a deep blue sky. Although the skeleton does not stand properly on the ground, and indeed his whole posture looks awkward and unnatural, he nevertheless manages to look much more three-dimensional than the diagrams of the *Figura incisionis* series. Partly this is achieved by making him seem to inhabit a pictorial space, partly by having him look to his left rather than face straight ahead, centre of the eye was the seat of vision). One of these diagrams is reproduced here (Fig. 25), and shows how a geometrical idea provided the basis for understanding how the eye was constructed. The diagram is built up of a series of circles, the centres of which are marked not only by captions but also by the still visible pinpricks where the scribe used a drawing compass.

The circles themselves represent the tunics and humours of the eye. The line a – 1 represents the visible object, rays from which pass through the circles of the *consolidativa*, *cornea*, and *uvea*, before they strike the top surface (at *c* and *d*) of the centremost circle, which represents the crystalline humour at the middle of the eye. Instead of the rays going straight on to hit the centre point of the eye *b*, they are refracted at *c* and *d* and are directed on to the back of the eye, where they hit the optic nerve, and information about the object is passed on to the brain. This last part of the process is not shown in our diagram.

The whole conception is geometrical and abstract, governed by the refraction of lines at points on a circle rather than detailed knowledge of the structure of the eye. Bacon's theory was an elaborate attempt to reconcile what Aristotle had said about layers in the structure of the eye with a mathematical model of vision developed by the Arabs. But he was far more interested in the geometry of

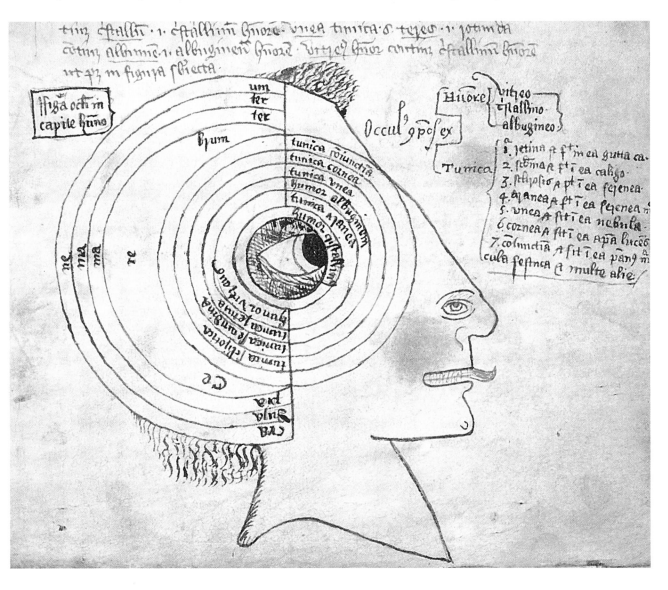

Fig. 26
Seven tunics and three humours of the eye are here represented, together with parts of the head (at the rear). Many of the terms for parts of the eye are still used. From the 'book of Macharias on the eye', late 14th - or early 15th-century. *BL, Sloane MS 981, f. 68*

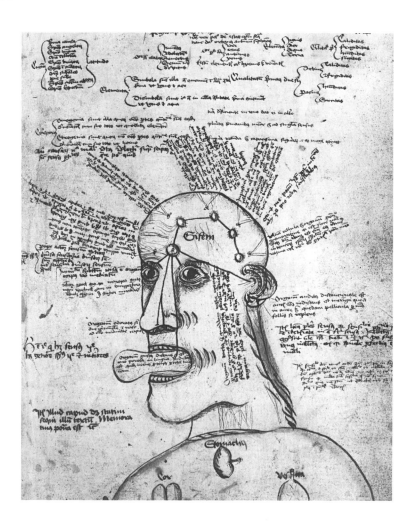

refraction than in the structure of the eye, and
his diagrams are good examples of the way in
which descriptive anatomy was subordinat-
ed to the demands of a deductive science with
higher claims to logical consistency.

By contrast, Fig. 26 accompanies an
anatomical rather than mathematical text, but
even so it could hardly be said to strive after
exactness. This diagram comes from a late
14th- or early 15th-century text which is headed 'the book of Macharias on the eye, called
Salaracer or secret of secrets'. As Zacharias
rather than Macharias, this author has been
tentatively identified with a 12th century
physician educated at Salerno, who may have
lived in Byzantium under Manuel I Com-
nenus (Emperor from 1143 to 1180). He
wrote a Latin treatise on eye diseases, in two
or three books. The anatomical text is very
short and describes the tunics and humours
of the eye. The diagram itself is headed 'Figure of the eye in the human head', and shows
these tunics and humours in schematic form.
The part played by the head is really more
ornamental than anatomical here, as the large
free-standing eye at the centre, the touches of

red on tongue and teeth, and the second eye
in the long nose, all suggest. But it does succeed in giving a rather dull diagram a fine
surrealist air.

Unlike the Bacon diagram, a full range of
seven tunics and three humours is represented, and the eye as a whole is divided much
more decisively into front and rear sections.
In the front or right side of the eye we see that
the humours and tunics, with the exception
of the crystalline humour at the centre, are
named differently from the semi-circles in the
rear or left side. Behind the eye itself is the *cere-
brum*, which is encased (reading from inside
to out) by the *pia mater* (soft membrane), *dura
mater* (hard membrane), and *cranium*. Along
side the diagram is a verbal breakdown of the
eye structure, but this time each part is tied to
a specific eye disease associated with it. This
diagram is about as close to realism as the
medieval anatomists of the eye were prepared
to go – their aim was schematic, not realistic,
even when dealing with medical conditions of
the eye. However it is worth noting that many
of the terms used by these texts and diagrams
are still in use today for parts of the eye (con-
junctiva, vitreous, crystalline, sclerotic, etc.).

The same could be said of the terms which
occur in another very popular sort of anatomical drawing. The human sensorium and faculties of the mind were all allotted specific
regions in the brain in medieval philosophy,
coinciding more or less with the ventricles or
cavities as described by Galen (anterior, median, and posterior, together with the hypoph-
ysis or pituitary cavity). One example of this
scheme can be found in a Wellcome manuscript written, and perhaps provided with a
commentary, by the German historian Johann
Lindner at Leipzig from 1472 to 1474 (Fig.
27). Lindner chose a series of Aristotelian and
other texts on logic and natural philosophy
to copy; the purpose of the drawing is to
encapsulate scholastic doctrine on the classification and localisation of external and internal senses. The captions refer to Avicenna and
Aquinas as authorities, but the arrangement
shown is probably drawn from Albertus Mag-
nus, who tied sensory and mental powers into
a basically Galenic picture of the physical
structure of the brain.

This particular drawing stands out from others of the same type by the energy of its line, free from any constraint imposed by truth to appearance. The tongue, like other external organs of sense (eyes, ears, and nose), is shown connected by lines to the *sensorium commune*, in the first compartment of the anterior ventricle of the brain. The connecting lines do not stand for vessels of any observable kind, but are imaginary links called for by the theoretical connection between sense and thought. The *sensorium commune* (a distant ancestor of our 'common sense') is where the information obtained from the sense organs is assimilated and basic comparisons made. There are captions alongside explaining the working of the different external senses, or – in the case of taste – written on the face behind the mouth.

The remaining ventricles of the brain are occupied (from front to back) by cells containing the internal senses of imagination, fantasy, estimation, and memory – corresponding very roughly to the faculties we would understand by these terms, though given a much more technical meaning in scholastic philosophy. These internal senses do not work directly on data provided by the external senses, but on secondary ideas derived from it. At the foot of the picture, on the upper part of the chest, appear crude and displaced outlines of the heart, stomach, and bladder. These are all suggested by reductions of shape which would be recognised immediately by the viewer. They are probably meant to remind him of the other vital organs of the body, besides the brain. The scheme as a whole is intended as an aid to the visualising of philosophical concepts, rather than as a guide to medical practice.

The oldest attested tradition of anatomy illustration in the Middle Ages, for which one manuscript survives from the 9th century, is gynaecological, or rather obstetrical. In a 9th-century manuscript in the Royal Library of Brussels are thirteen drawings of the foetus in different positions within a flask-shaped womb. The foetus is shown always as a fully grown *homunculus* or little man, not as a true baby. As well as containing a variety of birth

Fig. 28
Foetal presentations. The last five in the series of seventeen positions, showing two cases of twins. (Number 17 at far right may actually be a repeat of number 13 at far left.) There is no indication here of where the baby is supposed to emerge from the womb. From a 15th-century English manuscript. *BL, Sloane MS 2463, f. 218v*

positions, the series of wombs hold any number of figures up to eleven! The illustrations go with a text of Moschion's *Gynaecia* ('Gynaecology'), written originally probably in the 6th century, but based in its turn on the writings of Soranus of Ephesus, who practised in Rome about 100 AD. It is possible that the drawings too may go back as far as Soranus himself, if not further. Quite a number of other later manuscripts in this tradition survive, together with the same series of drawings, but increased in number to sixteen. Eventually they achieved a wide circulation, for they were copied in printed books right through to the 17th century. Two 15th-century manuscripts in this tradition are in the British Library, and their illustrations closely resemble one another. They share the peculiarity of having a series of *seventeen* figures – it looks as if the thirteenth in the series has been repeated with a slight variation for the seventeenth (Fig. 28). Numbers 5 – 8 in the series are shown from the other manuscript in Fig. 29.

In these manuscripts the original flask shape has changed into a simple sphere, painted with a rose-coloured wash. The cherubic figures inside adopt a sequence of fanciful poses, rotating all the way through 360°. Fig. 29 is notable for the suggestion of a mouth to the womb at the bottom of the circle. This is anatomically accurate enough to suggest that the painter or his instructor knew something about the matter. In both the British Library manuscripts the pictures are interspersed in groups of four or five in the middle of an English translation of a gynaecological treatise extracted from the *Rogerina*, a 13th century work on practical medicine by one Roger Baron. (The chapter on delivery does not come from the *Rogerina*, however, and is of unknown origin).

The text does deal with sixteen 'unnatural' positions in childbirth, for which the remedy is usually to try to rotate the child manually to the 'natural' position of head first, with arms alongside the legs. However the various positions described in the text do not correlate neatly with the drawings, which confirms the suspicion that the two did not always belong together. Numbers 15 and 16 in the series display twins, one pair upright in the womb, the other head down. It is not at all clear from the text what the obstetrician should do if both twins descend together, as the illustrations suggest (Fig. 28). Despite the incongruity of text and illustration, the same series seems to have exerted a hold on the medical imagination from the early centuries AD to the 17th century.

Just as today, to the ancient anatomists the study of anatomy was unthinkable without the practice of dissection. Often it is true they could only carry out dissections of animals like the ape or the pig, and had to argue from similarities in structure to the human case. But, contrary perhaps to our expectations, dissection of the human corpse was not banned in the Middle Ages, though it was normally carried out under strict official regulation. The first well-documented cases of dissection we know of occurred at the beginning of the 14th century at Bologna, in the famous medical school there. Many of these dissections were really autopsies carried out for forensic purposes – to enable the surgeon to pronounce on allegations of poisoning or cases of assault. Anatomical dissection for teaching purposes seems to have been

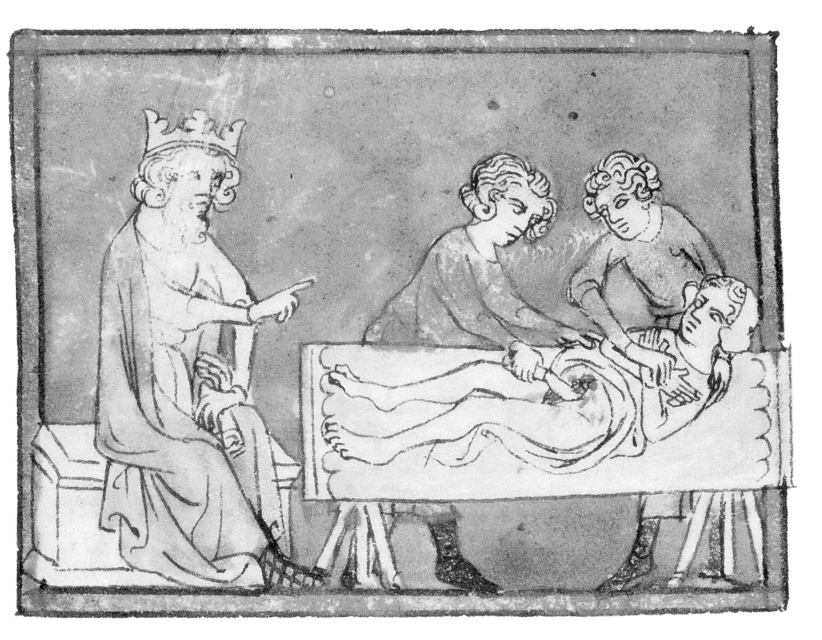

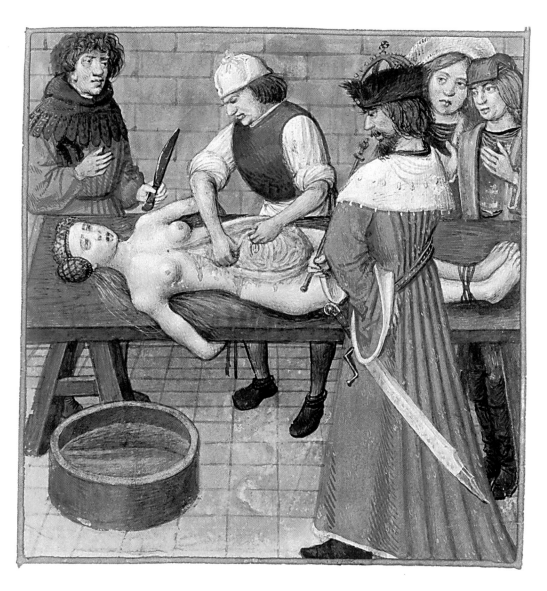

the Middle Ages are not intended to instruct the viewer in techniques or further his anatomical knowledge in any way, but simply to help tell a good story.

One of the most popular topics for the illustration of dissection was the story of how Nero ordered his mother Agrippina to be dissected before him in order to satisfy his unnatural curiosity as to where he came from. This story is found in manuscripts of the *Roman de la Rose*, and is illustrated here by a Flemish example of about 1500 (Fig. 31). This particular picture differs from most of its kind by introducing a note of realism (compare Fig. 30). Of course all the characters are dressed in contemporary clothes: Nero is in a long gown decorated with fleur-de-lys, with a sceptre in his hand, an imperial crown on his head, and a sword at his side. Behind him stand two courtiers. But the dissector himself has his sleeves rolled up in a most business-like fashion, while his assistant holds out a knife in a purposeful way. Agrippina lies on a trestle table wearing a 15th-century hair-net, and has her feet tied together, with her hands also tied under the table. There is a bowl of water on the floor to catch blood and dissected matter. Most pictures of dissection, and this one is no exception, show a longitudinal section from breast bone to pubic bone. Here the realism ends, for the intestines shown are not painted with any attempt to register detail. The illustrator's attention to practical matters suggests a certain familiarity with the tools and procedures of dissection, though no particular interest in internal anatomy. The main function of a picture like this was to shock the viewer with Nero's cold-blooded matricide, and his obscene curiosity. We should not read into it an indictment of the practice of dissection itself.

Fig. 31
Nero watches with curiosity as his mother Agrippina is dissected. A favourite story for medieval illuminators (compare Fig. 30), this example is untypical in its realistic approach to instruments and furniture, if not anatomy. From a Flemish manuscript of the *Roman de la Rose*, c.1500.
BL, Harley MS 4425, f. 59

concentrated on animals in the early Middle Ages; but at least one book the *Anatomia* of Mondino de' Liuzzi, written in 1316 or 1317, was meant to act as a guide to the dissection of the human cadaver. The use of dissection for teaching purposes did not mean of course that research based on observations made on these occasions replaced the anatomical doctrines of Galen – far from it, they were used to illustrate Galenic anatomy rather than to investigate. No continuous tradition of anatomical illustration grew up as a result of scholastic use of dissection for teaching purposes, and as a consequence, we find very few scenes of anatomical dissections in medical manuscripts. The vast majority of the pictures of dissection which survive from

DIAGNOSIS AND PROGNOSIS

If the physician of the Middle Ages had a badge of office, it was surely the jordan, or urine glass. He is portrayed so often in miniatures holding the jordan up to the light as to be instantly recognisable by what he carries. Sometimes, as in the famous Ellesmere Chaucer manuscript, he is even seen carrying the glass on horseback. Encyclopaedic works which begin with a discussion of the division of the sciences also occasionally symbolise medicine in the same way. In a full-page miniature from an early 14th-century manuscript of the *Tresor* ('Treasury') of Brunetto Latini (Fig. 32), probably executed in the south of France, we can see 'fisique' placed below canon law ('decres') and above civil law ('lois') in a column showing different professional activities, with their attributes. Even without the patient with his bandaged head and stick, we would know this was medicine rather than natural science (physics) because the physician holds a urine glass. He is shown sitting down, and dressed in long robes, to establish his status as a professional or learned man, and he points to the flask – presumably in the course of diagnosing the patient's illness. This, then, is how the physician looked to his contemporaries outside the medical profession (see Fig. 33).

The urine glass did not become the symbol of a physician's office by accident; it was

Fig. 32
The profession of medicine ('fisique') in its place above civil law, and below canon law, in a column from a full-page miniature in the *Trésor* of Brunetto Latini (an early 14th-century manuscript). The physician is examining a urine glass.
BL, Additional MS 30024, f. 1v

Fig. 33
The calendar for August, with a vignette of a physician examining urine at the bedside. Written by Antonio Sinibaldi, illuminated by Francesco Rosselli, in Lorenzo de' Medici's Book of Hours.
Florence, Biblioteca Laurenziana, MS Ashb. 1874, f. 8

because the inspection of urine played such an important part in medieval diagnosis. In classical times a great deal of attention had been devoted to a whole range of physical signs and observations of the most minute detail, as the surviving corpus of Hippocratic writings tell us. This sort of diagnosis was only a preliminary to a declaration of the patient's future prospects, often made in public. The skilled physician could make his reputation by accurately foretelling the course of an illness. Prognosis also allowed the physician to modify his therapy in the light of whatever harmful changes he foresaw in individual cases. Later authors, and in particular Galen, linked diagnosis and prognosis to a disease theory based on changes in the balance of the four humours (blood, phlegm, black bile, and yellow bile), signified to the physician by changes in urine or pulse.

As we have seen, short tracts on diagnosis from urine or pulse were among the first writings to be translated from Arabic into Latin in the Middle Ages, and formed part of the *articella* or university curriculum (see pp. 21-24). The mass of physical observations contained in the Hippocratic writings were not accessible, so detailed monitoring of a variety of different signs was neglected in favour of concentration on diagnosis by urine and pulse alone. These forms of diagnosis relied on fine discriminations of type, in which the physician demonstrated his expertise, rather than on building up a picture of the patient's illness from every physical sign or symptom described by the patient. Inspection of urine seems to have weighed more with medieval physicians than pulse, though with the ancients it had been the other way round. Byzantine authors of the 4th century had already done the work of constructing a basic system of notation to capture the distinctions between urine specimens, whereas this was much more difficult for pulse. Running a

poor third to these other methods in popularity was the analysis of samples of blood, which developed from the practice of regular blood-letting. It seems to have been a relative latecomer on the scene, for it was never part of the basic university syllabus in medicine, and few references to it can be found before the 15th century.

Medieval physicians did not always distinguish sharply between symptoms (that is, physical signs and what the patient complained of) and the disease or condition from which he suffered. The description of particular diseases often amounted to no more than a list of the symptoms with which it was associated. Theoretical explanation of the causes and development of disease (aetiology) played a limited role in medieval medicine, to judge by the writings which are left to us. Many diseases could after all be reduced conceptually to changes in the balance of the humours, and therapy could proceed on the basis of attempting to recover that balance.

This trend against disease theory was accelerated by the endless re-arranging and digesting of authorities in medical texts as time went by. Each new digest tended to neglect the theoretical element in favour of practical therapy, and in extreme cases this could reduce a text to lists of symptoms and appropriate cures. This was not the result of intellectual laziness, but of an effort to present the information contained in books in a form that could be consulted easily, perhaps even in the course of diagnosis itself.

Probably one of the things that made uroscopy such a favourite tool of diagnosis was that the distinctions it depended upon could be made visible in the shape of coloured diagrams. These diagrams of urine glasses survive in large numbers in medieval manuscripts, and the fact that so many of them are crude and amateurish in design shows that they were useful working tools in diagnosis, not just surplus decoration. Traditionally there were twenty or so distinctions of colour, usually

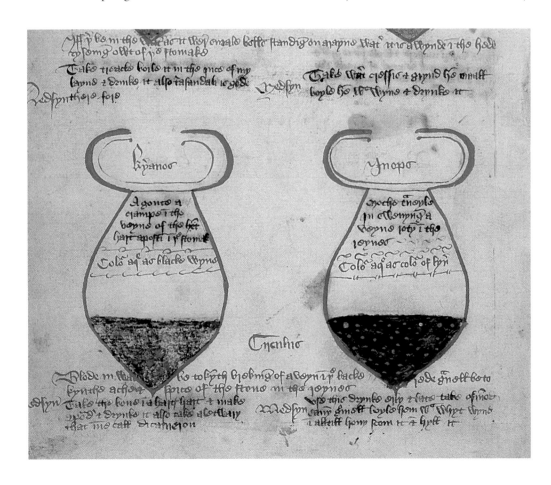

Fig. 35
Jordans (urine glasses), from the twenty described in an English 15th-century manuscript. They show different bands of colour as well as floating particles at various levels. The Greek terms for the colours are *kyanos* (blue) and *inopos* (wine-coloured).
BL, Sloane MS 7, f. 59v

45

represented by twenty separate drawings. Sometimes they were arranged in rows, or even circles. A typical English example from the 15th century, with four urine glasses to a page, is seen in Fig. 35. Here are two of the glasses, the mouth of the jordan seen as if from above, the body in vertical section.

This manuscript preserves remarkably well the basic distinction relied on by uroscopy, colour. The left-hand glass is labelled *kyanos* or blue, the right hand *inop[o]s* or wine-coloured, and although in the manuscript the blue has faded to grey, the liverish-red colour still comes up fresh. The Greek names for the colours are glossed with an English equivalent. So *kyanos* is said to be 'as black wyne', and *inop[o]s* 'as colour of liver'. The diagrams refine the twenty basic colour distinctions further by showing how a band of a different shade of colour may be found at the top of the urine sample, or how particles float in the urine. In the left-hand glass there is a reddish band at the top of the grey-blue area, and a few splashes of red near the bottom to indicate spots of blood. In the right-hand glass there are smaller spots of red spattered throughout the sample.

The captions explain the significance of these distinctions. To each basic colour is assigned a very abbreviated list of common illnesses with which it is associated. Thus *kyanos* could mean a gout, a cramp in the vein of the heart, or an abscess in the stomach. The caption for what is called the 'circle' (here written in red) explains the meaning of the finer distinctions – 'blood in water betokeneth breaking of a vein in the back of the head; gravel betokeneth ache and spite of the stone in the reins (kidney)'. Below this, at the bottom of the page, a suitable medicine is prescribed: for the ailments associated with *kyanos* the text suggests making a compound of the bone in the heart of a hart (?), or an electuary which men call 'dicameron'. This sort of diagnostic and therapeutic information supposes a familiarity with disease terminology and medicines to which we are no longer privy.

Although the principle of diagnosis by uroscopy was simple enough, there were enough variables to allow much fine discrimination in practice. We know that some physicians with a great reputation for their skill in uroscopy used to give their verdict on jordans brought to them for analysis, without ever seeing the patient. A number of pictures show a messenger arriving at the physician's door carrying a special little basket for holding the urine glass with its sample. Uroscopy did after all offer the prospect of arriving at a diagnosis based on observable distinctions which could be expressed in a colour diagram – its criteria were objective rather than merely subjective. This helps to explain the credibility it retained for centuries to come.

Diagnosis by pulse could not of course be so easily reduced to a visual scheme. The only visual materials we have that tell us about the practice of taking the pulse in the Middle Ages are scenes of physician and patient, some of which give an idea of how a diagnosis was made. One of the more mysterious of such scenes is Fig. 37. This comes from a manuscript from the Arundel collection in the British Library containing a number of short tracts in Latin and German, some of which date from the 13th century, others from the 14th. Curiously the manuscript does not contain any treatise on pulse, and on the back of the single folio on which our picture occurs there is only a short tract on the purgative powers of the plant colocynth. Why should this unusually fine picture, with its gold background, and the minute attention paid to light and shade in the folds of the garments, be found in such a workmanlike manuscript? Are the figures meant to represent anybody in particular? These questions still await an answer.

Unfortunately the picture's surface has been damaged to some extent by rubbing, but it is still possible to appreciate the delicate colouring, the stately composition and the grave faces of the figures, the whole having strong overtones of the German Romanesque style of religious art. Note too the curious box cuffs on one sleeve of each figure. Both doctor and female patient seem to be fairly advanced in age, and sit together on a bench. The doctor holds the fingers of the patient's left hand in his left, while he has placed four fingers on the radial artery, in a manner approved by classical and modern authorities alike. The gesture the patient makes with her right hand suggests that she is describing her symptoms to the attentive physician. We may suppose that whoever bound this single leaf into the medical compendium thought it an inspiring and instructive vision of the physician's role.

As in the case of uroscopy, the well-trained physician had a complex body of signs to look for in the pulse. Galen had already distinguished at least twenty-seven varieties of pulse, and his Arab and Latin commentators agreed in identifying the main ways of classifying pulse (by strength/weakness, regularity/irregularity, etc.). They had also identified a large number of 'special' pulses, some of which suggest that ancient and medieval physicians were highly sensitive to minute distinctions of pulse by touch, trying to express those distinctions by analogy – for instance, 'gazelle-like' or 'ant-like' are Galen's own terms for two of these special pulses. Variations in pulse could be ascribed to a whole range of factors, from climate to age, sex, and mental state of the patient, as well as to particular disease conditions. Without a clear understanding of the action of the heart as a pump, or of the relationship between the behaviour of pulse and the functioning of other bodily processes, the medieval physicians nevertheless made it the touchstone of the general state of health of the body. It is a measure of the powers of their discrimination that some of the symptomatic pulses they identified were still used in diagnosis up to the introduction of the electrocardiograph.

Bloodletting offered the opportunity for a third major method of diagnosis – observing blood samples given by the patient. In the course of bloodletting the practitioner needed to tell, by the colour and consistency of the blood, when it was time to staunch the flow. From this it would have been a short step to using the blood to make a diagnosis. Taste, smell, and heat were added to the other telling factors, and observations were made as the blood flowed, as it was clotting, and once it was fully caked. The blood was some-

Fig. 36
Four 14th-century
scenes from Rhasis,
Ad Almansorem,
in an Italian translation
by Zucchero de'
Bencivenni. The right
hand scenes show
Rhasis examining
urine (above),
and pulse (below).
*Florence,
Biblioteca Laurenziana,
MS Plut. 73.43, f. 6v*

Fig. 37
Taking the pulse.
The position of
the physician's fingers
on the left wrist is
in accordance with
the best medieval
and modern practice.
This single picture does
not appear to have any
connection with
the rest of the medical
treatises in which
it is found.
It was probably made
in Germany in the late
13th century.
BL, Arundel MS 295,
f. 256

trestle table, upon which are placed another eleven dishes of blood. The short German text which goes with the picture does not explain why there should be twelve dishes so neatly arranged, but does give twenty nine different diagnoses based on all the combinations of factors mentioned above. Haematoscopy (as we should call it today) was not necessarily practised only by the qualified physician, but also by the surgeon, barber, or bath attendant. These lesser practitioners had opportunity for this kind of diagnosis, because letting blood was never the exclusive preserve of university-trained physicians. Here the picture itself does not play the part of a diagnostic tool, but just gives us a glimpse of how a contemporary artist visualised the scene.

In the eyes of illustrators, physicians were more often diagnosticians than dispensers of forms of treatment. We can see this in non-medical as well as medical books. In the margins of many medieval manuscripts we find images of animals and grotesques which have nothing to do with the subject of the text. Among the animal inhabitants of this world, the ape and fox are the most prominent. Both these animals act out the part of men, but of men given over to passion and appetite rather than governed by reason. This inverted view of the natural order of things serves to amuse but also to remind the viewer of the foibles of humanity. The escapades of ape and fox often hold up a sardonic mirror to medicine in this way: the ape is frequently shown examining a jordan with a judicious air. He appears several times in the margins of the Smithfield Decretals, for instance – a manuscript of the canon-law edicts of Pope Gregory IX, written in Italy, but illuminated in England, in the second quarter of the 14th century (later owned by St Bartholomew's priory of Smithfield, on the site of the present hospital in London).

Besides the ape, the stories of Reynard the Fox seem to have provided direct inspiration for a number of pictures in the Smithfield Decretals. In Fig. 39 we see a particularly sly-looking fox taking the pulse of a recumbent wolf. The wolf is bandaged about the head, and on the next page (Fig. 40) the fox is seen

times washed through a cloth as to isolate impurities, which were important in diagnosis. But the most essential tools for the purpose were a number of beakers or dishes in which to hold the blood, so that samples could be compared as well as observed individually. Sometimes these dishes, smaller than those used simply for catching blood as it was let from the patient, can be identified in pictures, but actual scenes of diagnosis from blood samples are very hard to find.

One fine example from Germany, which we know was completed in 1446, is Fig. 38. A man with a pointed hat, presumably a physician, and perhaps Jewish, holds out a dish towards a woman, who might be a patient or an assistant. The previous picture in the same manuscript shows a man taking blood from a woman's arm, so probably she is the patient of our picture. They stand behind a

Fig. 38
Haematoscopy
(blood diagnosis)
was practised with samples
obtained from blood-letting.
Taste, smell, and heat
were used as indicators,
and samples were taken
as the blood flowed, as it was
clotting, and after it was fully
caked. From a German
15th-century manuscript.
*BL, Additional MS 17987,
f. 101*

Fig. 40
Reynard the Fox takes his
leave of his victim, the wolf.
*BL, Royal MS 10 E IV,
f. 54v*

Fig. 39
Reynard the Fox takes the pulse
of a wolf. From the lower margin
of the Smithfield Decretals,

a 14th-century collection of the edicts
of Pope Gregory IX.
BL, Royal MS 10 E IV, f. 54

taking his leave of the wolf, who this time is flat on his back with his legs in the air. One story about Reynard the Fox tells how he is summoned to the court of Noble the Lion who lies sick, and is told that only Reynard can cure him. On the way to court, Reynard steals the magic herb *aliboron* with the pouch of a sleeping pilgrim. Reynard tells Noble that he needs the skin of Reynard's enemy the wolf to wrap him in, as part of the cure. In Fig. 39 we see Reynard with the staff and pouches of a pilgrim, although in the interest of consistency he ought really to be taking the pulse of Noble the Lion, not the wolf. The skinned wolf on the next page (Fig. 40), on the other hand, is entirely appropriate to the story. Even in the world turned upside down, let us note, it is diagnosis that attracts the illustrator as a subject for his art.

In scenes of consultation between physician and patient, illustrators did however sometimes widen the definition of diagnosis beyond uroscopy and pulse-taking. An extraordinary series of pictures of such consultations is to be found in a manuscript illuminated in an Amiens workshop of the early 14th century. The whole series of forty-eight scenes prefaces a French translation of the herbal of Matthew Platearius, known as *Circa instans* from the first words of the Latin text. Normally illustrated herbals are, by definition almost, pictures of the herbs and plants described, but here the series of pictures has no direct relation to the text, which is in alphabetical order of plant names. Instead the pictures show consultations concerning a variety of different symptoms, and are arranged, but very carelessly, in head to toe order of symptom. They could not have helped anyone consulting the text of the herbal, or directed the viewer to remedies for the symptoms shown. Perhaps they were originally intended to accompany a treatise of practical medicine rather than a herbal, although even then they could not be used as a programme of instruction in techniques of diagnosis. They are more a sort of visual record of cases with which physicians and surgeons might be confronted in the consulting room wherever that might be.

Fig. 42 shows four of the forty-eight scenes. The first is clear enough – a picture of a patient vomiting in the presence of the physician. At

Fig. 41
The physician touches the child's stomach to find if it feels hard. From a 12th-century south Italian manuscript of the Pseudo-Apuleius herbal, based on a Byzantine model. *Florence, Biblioteca Laurenziana, MS Plut. 73.16, f. 29v.*

top right we are shown a patient fainting or passing out, as he falls to his left. At bottom left, a patient opens his mouth and bares his teeth, presumably to suggest he has toothache. The fourth picture shows a patient who points to his hair, which is not wavy with a fringe, as in the other scenes, but seems to be unusually crinkly. None of these features depicted by the artist can be linked directly to a specific disease or ailment, and perhaps we should think of them as pictures of symptoms rather than clinical signs – that is to say, reflecting the patient's own view of his ailment and not the physical signs which physicians interpret as the result of disease states. Elsewhere in the series we are shown nosebleeds, rashes, swellings, etc., but in some we see just the doctor and the patient in conversation, with no indication of symptoms. These last scenes are perhaps best interpreted as a sort of silent equivalent of the patient's own description of his symptoms. In only one picture of the whole forty-eight does the doctor actually do more than gesture; here he touches the forehead of a patient.

It is worth noting that one of the physicians shown here – in the toothache scene – wears a surgeon's cap, and an armless gown, rather than the robes of a doctor of physic. Perhaps this is because dentistry fell into the province of the surgeon rather than the physician.

The Greeks had made diagnosis subservient to prognosis – whereas a diagnosis told you only what the state of health was at a given instant, the art of prognosis told you the likely future outcome of an ailment, and the effect that certain treatments would have on it. In the Middle Ages, however, prognosis assumed a rather different significance, less to do with the natural course of specific diseases, and more to do with the personal fate of the individual. This fate in turn was bound up with external influences like the conjunctions of the planets. Not that it was a case of Greek rational medicine being replaced by medieval superstition. For one thing the Greeks pioneered many of the general prognostic devices which medieval man used, and for another the astrological element was extremely 'rational' insofar as it depended upon precise observations and causal explanations of the interaction of macrocosm and microcosm .

Prognostic devices in the shape of diagrams were handed down by the Greeks (and before this perhaps by the Egyptians). When they were not just written out as a series of instructions, they probably began as plain diagrams, rather like the modern horoscope. Later, purely pictorial and decorative elements crept in, probably before the Latin versions made from the 8th century onwards. At any rate, in early Anglo-Saxon diagrams of the 'Sphere of Apuleius', one of the commonest of these devices, personifications of life and death have become an integral part, along with the necessary formulae. The 'Sphere of Apuleius'

Fig. 42
Four of the forty-eight scenes of consultations between doctor and patient which preface an early 14th-century book of medicinal simples. We see vomiting, fainting toothache, and a hair problem, but there are no clues as to the diseases which they signify.
BL, Sloane MS 1977, f. 50v

occurs amongst a group of other tables for computing dates of equinoxes, solstices, and movable feasts (particularly Easter), which preface Anglo-Saxon psalters. One of the best examples, though far from the earliest, may be found in the Tiberius Psalter of the mid 11th century (Fig. 44).

The 'Sphere of Apuleius' is basically a device for foretelling the outcome of an illness – whether the patient will live or die. All that is needed is a table of the alphabet, with each letter assigned a numerical value. Then for each letter of the patient's name a number can be read off, and to the total is added the day of the moon on which the patient fell sick. The final total is then divided by thirty, and the remainder is found either among the numbers signifying life, or among those signifying death. These last numbers are usually ranged round a sphere, the top half of which represents life, the bottom half, death. Sometimes each hemisphere is divided into three parts, one third representing a rapid recovery (or death), one third a moderate delay, and one third a protracted recovery (or death).

In Fig. 44 life and death are personified, and each carries in outstretched hands a long scroll on which the numbers are inscribed. Each scroll falls into three parts; these correspond to the forecast of delay in the outcome. The tables of letters with their numerical equivalents run down either side of the page. A caption runs round the outside of the whole scheme explaining how the Sphere is to be used.

Artistically this is a particularly fine image, despite the damage caused by the Ashburnham House fire of 1731, which ruined so many of Sir Robert Cotton's manuscripts. There are strong symbolic overtones in the image, since life is shown as a Christ figure touched with blue, and death as Satan, entirely outlined in brown. Satan has wings above his shoulders, but also six tiny dragons flying out on either side of his head: these represent the six sons of death mentioned in the apocryphal Coptic Book of the Resurrection of the Christ, held to be responsible for bringing sickness on us all. In terms of artistic style,

Satan's pose is settling into Romanesque stillness; in the Christ figure we can still see, in the exuberant energy of line in the folds of the garment, the debt which later Anglo-Saxon art owed to the Utrecht Psalter. This blend of the secular prognostic and Christian iconography bridges the gap between the two uses to which devices like the 'Sphere of Apuleius' were put. For medical purposes prognostics were used to decide when a patient should be treated (or perhaps left to die), or even which type of treatment to try. They were also used to test for virginity or pregnancy, and to forecast the sex of a child. But the church needed to know if the last sacraments should be given, and whether sudden death was likely. Right through into the 16th century, we find the same devices in both secular and religious manuscripts, differing only in the uses to which they were put.

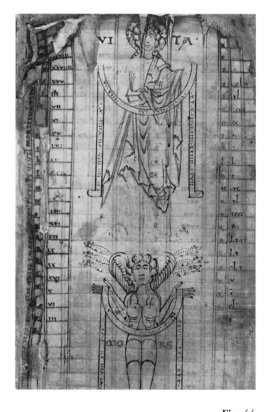

Medical and religious usage of the same instruments did not apply only in the field of prognostics. In the 15th century a fashion seems to have developed for the carrying of folded calendars, fastened by a tassel to the belt. Such calendars would have been handy tools of reference for churchmen or those laymen with an interest in astronomy and astrology. They consisted of a simple calendar of dates, tables of eclipses of the sun and moon for half a century ahead, as well as information which allowed calculation of when the moon would be in a particular astrological 'house'. But this information would have been useful to physicians too, especially if it was combined with other handy reference tools like rules for bloodletting, tables of urine glasses, a zodiac man, and a 'Sphere of Apuleius'. It would have given him much greater professional mobility, in that he had no need to bring the patients to his books, or the books to his patients, but could pay house-calls. Despite the heavy wear such folding calendars must have suffered, a surprising number of them have survived, and several of the type adapted for the physician are now in the British Library and the Wellcome Library.

In terms of physical construction, the folded calendars are relatively simple, yet strong and easy to consult. They are made of six or more small pieces of parchment, folded together across the middle, then folded again into sections (Fig. 45). Sewn together at the bottom, the sections are then gathered into an oblong shape. Each section is identified on the outside by a title, so that the relevant part can be quickly picked out and unfolded. Being made of parchment, they do not easily fray or tear. Despite this highly functional quality, they are also quite handsomely decorated, not only with ornamental initials but with diagrams of the eclipses, using gold, as well as illuminated bloodletting and zodiac men, and coloured tables of urine glasses. They were obviously owned with pride, and not just regarded as working tools.

Fig. 46 shows one section of a calendar opened, demonstrating the two vertical folds. Not included in this photograph is another 'Sphere of Apuleius' on the same leaf. We see only the table of urines, which in this exam-

ple is finely coloured, and not much faded. The captions have muddled the usual reading at the top right of the table – giving the oriental rather than the occidental crocus in the description of *subrufus. Subrufus* should in any case be *subrubeus*, 'somewhat reddish', not 'somewhat brownish'. Whether this would have made much difference in diagnosing different ailments is hard to judge. The owner – it would be nice to know who he or she was – may well have been able to correct for scribal errors on the basis of what he knew already.

Another important picture element in these calendars is the zodiac man. Usually the signs of the zodiac are represented on the different parts of the body over which they hold particular influence (Aries – the head; Pisces – the feet, etc.). Sometimes (but not in the calendar) a mannikin stands at the centre of astrological influences, shown by lines connected to his body. In the calendars the simpler form is preferred. The use of these zodiac men, which are found in hundreds of manuscripts, was primarily to tell the physician that when the moon was in a particular sign, it would be inauspicious to let blood or operate on the part of the body associated with that sign.

A considerable body of Arabic literature on astrology had been translated into Latin along with the medical texts since the 13th century, and western European medicine became increasingly preoccupied with astrology in

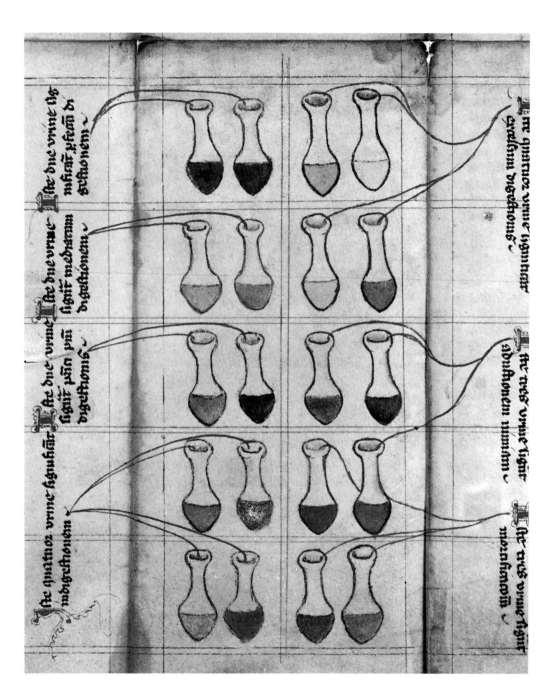

the 14th and 15th centuries, as it digested
and built on Arab foundations. The zodiac
man is only the most simplified and crude
statement of a complex body of theory built
on the influence of the stars of the zodiac on
the external parts of the body, and the planets on the internal. The medium through
which these astrological influences operated
was of course the movement of the four
humours. The moon, as the closest heavenly body, had the greatest influence on the
ebbing and flowing of these humours, as it
did over the tides. All this may be regarded
as a series of unjustifiable inferences from the
known facts about the heavens and about the
human body; but it had the backing of ancient
authority, as well as sophistication and
explanatory power. In these respects at least,
it was 'scientific' in one modern sense of that
term.

The zodiac man gave the artist every opportunity to indulge his fancy for the purely decorative, as well as conveying the basic information about influences on the body. Some
of the examples are illuminated, though many
more are just ink and wash. A nice example
from the 14th century, probably made in Germany, is Fig. 47. Here the outline work is in
black or red ink, with pen infilling as well as
wash. The cast of the face and the pose of the
figure are, as with so many of the anatomical figures of the Middle Ages, ecclesiastical
rather than secular in feel. There are some
idiosyncratic features about the signs of the
zodiac too – the crab (below the bull) looks
more like a lobster, while the scorpion (below
the scales) looks like a limbless dragon. The
goat is stag-like, and the twins (on either arm)
look like the Virgin. Aquarius is represented
by a water-jug. A later hand has added captions linking the signs to particular members
of the body. The text by the side of the head
deals with the use of music in soothing the
vital and animal spirits of man: it quotes Avicenna, the most famous of Arab medical
authors, in support of this practice.

Besides knowing which sign of the zodiac
corresponded to which part of the body, the
physician or surgeon would need to know
which sign the moon was moving through
on a given date. To do this he could make use

of tables, or he could use a volvelle – a device with one or more movable discs rotating within a fixed matrix. Sometimes these were beautifully chased in metal, and were also designed to function as astrolabes. They would have been highly treasured, although they tend now to tell us little about their owners, and the uses to which medical men, in particular, put them. But many volvelles were made of parchment, and one with a very definite medical connection survives in the Guild Book of the Barber-Surgeons of York. This book was written and illustrated for the Company of Barber-Surgeons in York, and perhaps even used professionally by the members. It contains, besides a variety of later additions, a series of drawings and schemes made in the late 15th century, of which the volvelle (Fig. 48) is one. Around the volvelle itself stand four figures drawn in the best Flemish style of the period, though probably done in England. At the top are Saints John the Baptist and John the Evangelist, patron saints of the Guild. At the bottom are Saints Cosmas and Damian, who were supposed to look after medicine and surgery respectively. Cosmas holds up a urine glass, making the familiar pointing gesture, while Damian holds a spatula with a lozenge-shaped head, ready to mix his medicines from the compartmentalised box.

The graduated circle which forms the matrix of the volvelle gives the days of the months on the outside (November is given 31 days), with the names and symbols of the months just inside. The degrees and signs of the zodiac are further in still, though the illustrator has managed to give Aries only 25° instead of 30° (one twelfth of 360°). Next we come to the movable disc which has a long finger attached. This is the part known as the index of the sun, because the surgeon could set it to the sign and degree of the zodiac through which the sun passed on any day of the year in which he was interested. The symbol of the sun is the gold band which runs inside this disc. But an important piece of the volvelle is missing – the index of the moon. This would have been a separate small rotatable disc at the centre, where a blank circle is now to be seen. It would have had a finger which extended at least as far as the degrees of the zodiac.

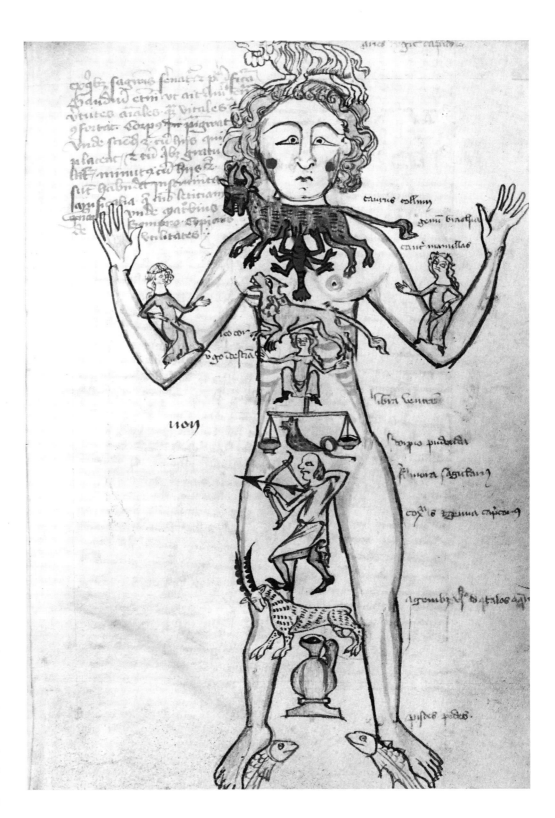

Fig. 47
A zodiac man. The signs of the zodiac which influence particular parts of the body are depicted in the appropriate places.

This information was used by the physician or surgeon as a guide to when operations or treatment would be safe and effective.

From a German 15th century manuscript.
BL, Arundel MS 251, f. 46

Fig. 48
The Barber-Surgeons'
volvelle. The moving
index of the volvelle
could be set at the sign
and degree of the
zodiac through which
the sun passed at
a given day. Saints
John the Baptist
and John
the Evangelist were
the patron saints
of the Guild
of Barber-Surgeons
of York, to whom this
manuscript belonged.
Saints Cosmas
and Damian were
the patron saints
of medicine
and surgery
*BL, Egerton MS 2572,
f. 51*

Having set his index of the sun at the correct date, the surgeon would have set the index of the moon at the number (written in red) on the larger rotating disc, corresponding to the age of the moon for the day concerned. Strictly there were only 29.5 days for a lunar month, but here we have a full 30. Finally the surgeon would have read off the zodiac sign and degree of the moon on the day concerned, with the help of the index of the moon. He would be able to determine in advance whether an operation or bloodletting would be auspicious; for example, if the part of the body operated on corresponded to the sign of the moon for that day, it would be most unwise to operate. Actually the mistakes we have seen in connection with the graduated circles of the matrix suggest either that the surgeons were not very fussy about accuracy in prognosis, or that this particular volvelle was not meant to be used in the course of practice.

Before leaving the subject of prognosis, we should not forget the *caladrius*, the mythical white bird which foretold recovery (by looking at the patient), or death (by turning its head away). This bird was supposed only to frequent the courts of kings, and in the bestiaries was made the vehicle of symbolic interpretation, in some cases identifying the *caladrius* with Christ himself, who turns His face towards the sinner whom He will save. It is possible that the *caladrius* was based on classical descriptions of a bird *icterus*, which was yellow but had the power of taking upon itself jaundice, known as the royal disease. In any case, its powers of prognosis were always the focus in illustrations of the *caladrius*, which are found not only in bestiaries, but in histories of Alexander the Great and other general encyclopaedic works.

Fig. 49 is taken from a 13th-century treatise on the significance of birds by Hugh of Folieto, which draws directly on the bestiary for its description of the *caladrius*. It shows two cases at once, one in which the *caladrius* looks at the patient, and one in which he looks away. As usual the *caladrius* is portrayed as a sea-bird, with webbed feet, though it does not resemble any real bird. The fixed staring eye of the bird is very prominent. The painting of the patient's face on the left has unfortunately become rather rubbed, but we can still see that he is looking back at the *caladrius* with a distinctly hopeful expression. The patient on the floor, however, looks most apprehensive, with a down-turned mouth – as well he might. The text adds, rather implausibly, that the marrow of the bird's femur is very good for treating diseases of the eye. First catch your *caladrius*.

Fig. 49
The *Caladrius* was a mythical white bird which attended the sick-bed of royalty, and foretold their recovery or death by looking at, or away from, the patient. Here are two different outcomes predicted in a 13th-century manuscript of the *Aviarium* of Hugh of Folieto. *BL, Sloane MS 278, f. 34v*

MATERIA MEDICA

From prehistory onwards, man has used the objects (animal, vegetable, and mineral), with which he shares the natural world, as instruments of healing. The practice of making pictures of these objects, whether for purposes of instruction or to use in magic, is probably almost as old. We know that by the first century BC pictures of plants had appeared in papyrus scrolls, the ancestors of the manuscript book. The elder Pliny, writing in the 1st century AD, mentioned plant illustration in his *Historia Naturalis* ('Natural History') though with some scepticism as to its usefulness:

. . . the subject has been treated by Greek writers, whom we have mentioned in their proper place; of these, Crateuas, Dionysius, and Metrodorus adopted a most attractive method, though one which makes clear little else except the difficulty of employing it. For they painted likenesses of the plants, and then wrote under them their properties. But not only is a picture misleading when the colours are so many, particularly as the aim is to copy nature, but beside this, much imperfection arises from the manifold hazards in the accuracy of copyists . . .

Pliny's last point holds good for the manuscript codex, as well as the papyrus scroll.

The Johnson Papyrus (see p. 14 and Fig. 50), which dates from about 400 AD, is the earliest surviving example in the West of an illustrated herbal. It depicts two herbs; 'simphyton', probably the common comfrey (*symphytum officinale* L.)*, and 'phlommos', perhaps mullein (*verbascum thapsus* L). Fig. 50 shows 'phlommos' or mullein, and the regular outline of the leaves, together with a certain formality in the composition as a whole, suggest that the artist was working from a previous exemplar rather than from the living plant. On the other hand, 'simphyton' or the common comfrey looks as if it might just have been drawn from life. Neither of the plants grows readily in the Nile valley, but the artist might have seen them on his travels. The legible fragments of Greek script indicate that the text of the herbal consisted of a description of the plant and of its medicinal uses. The book of which the papyrus is a leaf may well have been intended for a customer who could afford the best available. The coloured paintings, which have survived over a millennium and a half, required lavish use of colour and the services of a highly-skilled artist.

The Johnson Papyrus fills the gap between the Crateuas herbal mentioned by Pliny, and the Vienna Dioscorides of the 6th century AD. We know that copies of both the Dioscorides herbal and the Latin Pseudo-Apuleius herbal (whose comfrey picture looks very like the Johnson papyrus example), continued to be made in the 7th to 10th centuries AD. The story of the illustrated herbal is more obviously one of continuity between the Hellenistic and medieval periods than most other branches of medical illustration. Broadly speaking, the high quality of naturalism in a significant proportion of the Vienna Dioscorides pictures of plants, birds, snakes, reptiles, and mammals, was not matched again until the 15th century. Pliny's strictures on the baneful effects of copying seem to have been justified in the event. But we should not lose sight of two salient facts about medieval herbals. First, the vast majority of treatises on *materia medica* in the Middle Ages were not illustrated, and presumably did not need to be (see Fig. 51). Second, those illustrations that survive, though far from naturalistic, seem nevertheless to have served their practical purpose. Added to this, we should remember that the realm of *materia medica* embraced far more than just the vegetable kingdom, and sometimes these other substances were the subject of illustration too. Lovers of the woodcut herbal, who look back to manuscripts only for antecedents of the great 16th-century herbals of Brunfels or Fuchs or Dodoens, have tended to overlook these facts, and write the history of the illustration of *materia medica* as a slow but steady rise from the barbarous distortions of the Middle Ages to the full flowering of Renaissance naturalism. But if we look again at the manuscript illustrations of materia medica with a less prejudiced eye, and try to keep in view the wider perspective indicated by the facts above, it may be that we will see more than just a tale of steady degradation by copying.

* L. indicates the modern Linnaean name for a plant. Otherwise Latin plant names are those given in the manuscript referred to.

Fig. 51
A list of medicinal simples and quantities.
This text is decorated, but not illustrated.
No risk of confusion about the plant named.
Montecassino, Biblioteca Casinensis,
MS 225, pp. 82-3

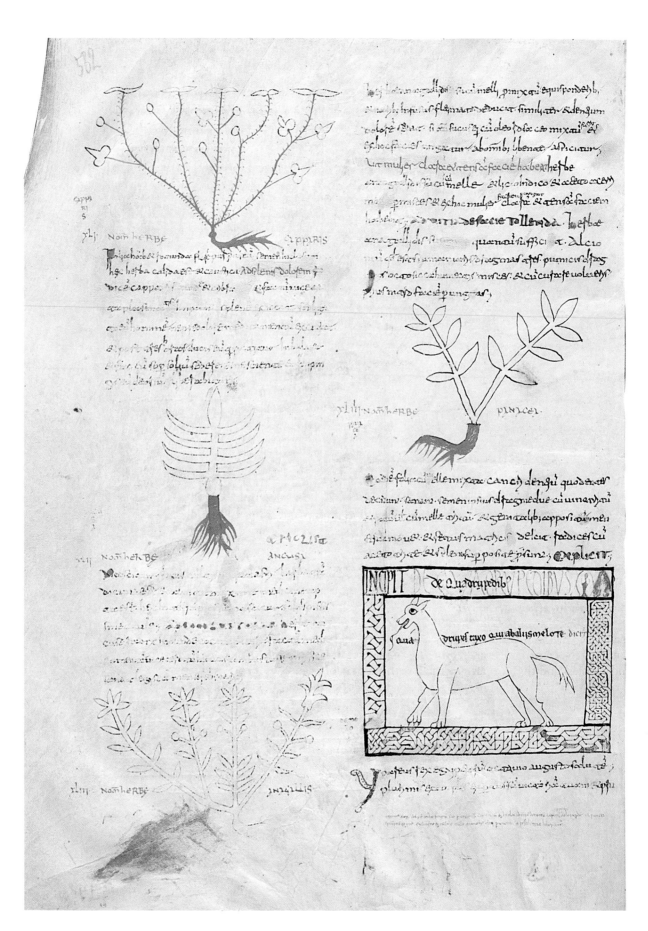

In the early Middle Ages, the most popular body of knowledge about *materia medica* was to be found in a complex of texts which included the herbal of Pseudo-Apuleius, Antonius Musa on the plant betony, a text on the medicinal use of the badger, another on the healing properties of the mulberry, and the *Medicina ex quadrupedis* ('Medicine from quadrupeds') of Sextus Placitus (see Fig. 52). The first and last of these were quite frequently illustrated, and one of the most splendid early examples of the illustrated tradition is a manuscript containing an Old English translation of these texts, made in England around 1050. Despite its being extensively damaged in the disastrous Ashburnham House fire of 1731, there are plenty of signs left in this manuscript that it was not just copied as a scholarly labour, but actually used. For instance, later hands have supplied captions to the plants and additional recipes. There is also a colour-keyed table of contents which allows the reader to find the recipes he wants from the ailments listed against each plant. Given the fact that the climate of northern Europe from the 9th to the 13th centuries was warmer and drier than it is now, some of the Mediterranean plants described in the original text of Pseudo-Apuleius (written in North Africa about the 5th century AD) may have flourished in the carefully cultivated medicinal gardens attached to monastic houses.

Apart from the dedication and author-presentation pages (see Fig.3), the illustrations of this manuscript fall into two main classes – the plants (interspersed with snakes, scorpions, and reptiles) and the animals proper. The snakes seem to have crept into what may have once been simply plant illustrations, probably because artists liked to dramatise the description of plants used against bites or stings. In our manuscript the scorpions are surprisingly realistic, despite the fact that even in Anglo-Saxon times the scorpion could not have been an English native. The plants themselves are rather stylised, but this need not have stopped them being useful to the would be gatherer or cultivator. Sometimes a more schematic illustration, which emphasises obvious distinctive features, gives a better idea of what to look for than an individualised plant portrait, particularly when, as here, the roots

are shown as well as the flower. However, most herbals got along without illustration, so we must assume that a lot of the lore involved in the recognition of plants was passed on by verbal or practical instruction, rather than by consulting books.

Fig. 53 shows *basilisca* or adderwort, and is one of the more obviously stylised of the plants in this manuscript. The leaves come at regular intervals on the straight stems, mostly opposite one another, though on one branch they occur alternately for part of its length. The flowers are little circles in shades of lilac and ruby. Each stem is brown, with light spots of white running up it to indicate roughness of texture. But the most striking feature is the root, wrapped about with a coil of serpents, which later hands have labelled adderwort and *basilisca*. In the text it says that *basilisca* or adderwort grows in the places where adders are, and that it is useful against three kinds of adder. Earlier on in the same text, another plant called adderwort is dealt with, one which we can identify with certainty as the modern snakeweed or bistort (*Polygonum bistorta* L.); this species of adderwort is supposed by the Oxford English Dictionary to receive its name from the coiling of its roots like snakes. Curiously the adderwort in Fig. 53 has made use of this pun, by showing the coils of snakes round the root. But the illustrator has not taken the other opportunity to pun by drawing the snakes each with a crown on its head, which in the Middle Ages was supposed to be the attribute of the legendary basilisk. There are at least three possible candidates for the modern equivalent of this adderwort – but the character of the illustration makes it impossible to be certain which one is meant.

The pictures of animals which illustrate the Sextus Placitus text on quadrupeds were probably never intended to aid recognition of the beasts. Familiar animals like the dog, ram, or boar, would need no introduction anyway; and the fanciful elephant, trunkless and covered with spots on a lozenge-shaped pattern of skin, would not have been much help, if help had been needed. The arrangement of the Latin text was not of much use to animal spotters either; the recipes come more or less

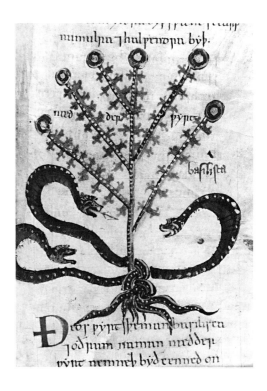

Fig. 53
The coiled snakes which form the roots give the plant depicted its English name – adderwort – though perhaps the adders should really be basilisks. From an Anglo-Saxon herbal, mid 11th century.
BL, Cotton MS Vitellius C III, f. 57

in the alphabetical order of the diseases they are intended to cure. The animal pictures are decorative in intent; there are very clear resemblances between the dog, the ram and the hare in our manuscript, and the drawings of the constellations which resemble these animals in contemporary manuscripts of the Aratus poem on the heavens. The artist obviously drew on an established tradition of animal illustration in Anglo-Saxon art, one which favoured lively poses and bright colours. Shown in Fig. 54 are the lion and the bull (the shrivelling of the fire-damaged vellum explains why the lion has lost part of his forehead). For the lion, the text says 'let those who suffer apparitions eat lion flesh; they will not after suffer any apparitions'.

For sore ears the text recommends lion's suet melted in a dish, and dropped in the ear. Lion's suet also works well on other kinds of sore. Of the bull it says 'against the dwelling by one of snakes, and for their removal; scatter a bull's horn burnt to ashes where the snakes dwell, they will flee away'. Bull's blood and bull's gall are also supposed to be good for various ailments of the head and face. The Anglo-Saxon text has boiled down the Latin original to the absolute essentials for treatment – the substances to be used and the ailments to be cured. The prosy parts and all irrelevant information have been pared away. This certainly argues that the text was copied for a practical purpose, even if we may doubt the effectiveness of most of the recipes.

Before leaving this manuscript, one last feature deserves notice; there are notes at the back by William Harvey, the English physician who discovered the circulation of the blood. His interest, too, seems to have been in the remedies offered by the text.

The Pseudo-Apuleius herbal and its companion texts were destined for a much longer life in Latin than in Anglo-Saxon, as a result of the Norman Conquest. There are a number of manuscripts surviving from the 12th century which include pictorial elements missing from the Anglo-Saxon manuscripts, and which apparently go back to very ancient sources. Although, as we shall see, the pictures as a whole are full of life, the plants

Fig. 54
The lion and the bull; two sources of medicines for a variety of ailments. From an Anglo-Saxon translation of Sextus Placitus, *Medicina ex quadrupedis*, mid 11th century. *BL, Cotton MS Vitellius C III, f. 81v*

Fig. 55
The centaur Chiron
and Aesculapius,
with herbs. From
a 9th century
manuscript
of the Pseudo-Apuleius
herbal.
Florence,
Biblioteca Laurenziana,
MS Plut. 73.41, f. 23

and animals themselves have become more stylised and schematic. Crowsfoot, the plant illustrated in Fig. 56 shows the Romanesque taste for a symmetrical display of branches and geometrical leaf forms. Crowsfoot is recommended for two ailments – dog-bite and nose-bleed (hence its other name, *sanguinaria*, or blood stauncher). Beneath the illustration of the herb there is an 'action scene'; a violent fight between a man and a dog is depicted, set against an architectural backdrop. The addition of 'action scenes' such as this obviously did little to enhance the herbal as a work of reference, but they certainly made the book more attractive to the casual reader. The origins of these pictorial additions go back to the late antique period, when many illustrations of technical or factual subjects seem to have been enhanced and dramatised in this way (see Fig. 55). The artists of this particular manuscript only occasionally got round to colouring the designs – the majority of the pictures are simply copied in ink outline only.

In some of the Anglo-Norman herbals (12th and early 13th century), the decorative potential of plants was exploited to an extent which could seriously have reduced their usefulness for plant identification. The designs become ever more symmetrical, the shapes of leaves and flowers more regular and uniform. The visual effect on the illuminated page was sometimes extremely beautiful, especially when the colours were supplemented by gold leaf or paint.

Fig 57 shows a *cameleia* (not the modern camellia, but wild teazle) from a 12th-century manuscript (see also p. 26). The decorative intention has been pushed further still, in this case, by the use of an ornamental backdrop of two shades of red and blue, speckled with white. There is also a rectangular double border which reminds us that we are dealing with purely two-dimensional rather than naturalistic values. The only calculated irregularity in the composition is the root, which is allowed to escape the rectangular prison of the frame. The *cameleia* itself is given ramrod-straight stalks, and even the hairs on leaf and flower march in regular order. However the characteristic prickly flowers and leaves

of wild teazle are still just about visible in this illustration .

According to the text, *cameleia* is effective against liver complaints, poisons, and in the cure of dropsy. The list of synonyms for *cameleia* used in different places seems to indicate some confusion. '*Corcodrillum*' for instance would seem to be *crocodileon*, a plant mentioned by Pliny, so called because of the rough skin of its stalk. However our plant has prickly leaves and flower heads but not a prickly stalk. Such exotic synonyms would not have been of much use to a herb-gatherer, though the learned physician might have been enterprising enough to look up what Pliny had to say about *crocodileon*.

(see also p. 26)

Fig. 57
Cameleia — not
the modern camellia,
but wild teazle —
is shown here.
The plant has become
an ornament to
the page in this
Anglo-Norman herbal
from the end
of the 12th century.
*BL, Sloane MS 1975,
f. 21*

Fig. 58
Male and female
mandrakes, from
a 7th-century Greek
manuscript of
Pseudo-Dioscorides,
Herbarium.
Naples,
Biblioteca Nazionale
Vittorio Emanuele II,
MS Gr.1 (ex Vindob.
Suppl. gr. 28), f. 90

While on the subject of exotics, the famous mandrake root offered the illustrator a splendid opportunity for visual drama. The mandrake was supposed to be fatal to any man who attempted to gather it, for he would be killed by its unearthly shriek as it was pulled from the ground. Only a dog could pull it up, with the aid of a chain, and the dog itself would die in the act Mandrakes resembled the human form, and there were two varieties, one masculine, one feminine (in fact probably the spring and autumn varieties). Fig. 59 represents the male mandrake being torn from the earth by a hound, who is shackled to the root by a chain. This particular illustration is noteworthy for the minute attention paid to the musculature and surface textures of the skin, as well as for the echo of a favourite theme of sacred art in this period – Christ trampling upon the beasts of hell. The manuscript in which it appears seems to have been written and illuminated in the region of the valley of the Meuse around 1175. But the model on which it was based probably came from southern Italy, where so many of the secular subjects that were illustrated in northern religious houses originated.

Other manuscripts of the Pseudo-Apuleius herbal show different parts of the story of the mandrake – men armed with iron tools setting out to hunt the mandrake, men attacking the root with their tools, or the aftermath, with both root and hound lying dead on the ground. The mandrake was credited with a variety of powers; Pseudo-Apuleius indicates that it counteracted diseases of the eye, spots on the body, serpent bites, pains in the joints, and many other ailments. The mandrake, which grows in the Near East, is known today to be poisonous, and its emetic and narcotic properties may well have been utilised in northern Europe. There was a significant trade in rare herbs and spices from the East early in the Middle Ages, in which the abbots of monastic houses are known to have dabbled. Thus the legends which grew up around the mandrake started with a real plant, an active medicinal agent which may have circulated more widely than might be suspected from its limited geographical range of origin .

In the animal kingdom, it was not only the large mammals featured in the bestiaries that were identified as sources of medicinal

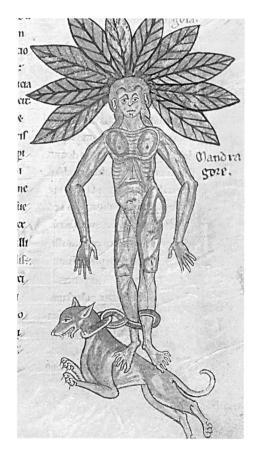

Fig. 59
A male mandrake is being torn from the ground
by a hound — the only way of uprooting this magic
plant. The real mandrake root does have emetic
and narcotic properties, and these may form the basis
of the great pharmacological powers attributed
to it in the Pseudo-Apuleius herbal.
From a Mosan manuscript of c.1175.
BL, Harley MS 1585, f. 57

simples. A whole range of smaller animals, reptiles and insects were also called upon. Normally these are represented, if at all, in a very careless and shorthand fashion – after all, such creatures rank very far down the ladder of creation. But there is one manuscript in the Wellcome Library which devotes minute attention even to the insect kingdom – almost certainly the only illustrated book of medicinal ingredients in the whole course of the Middle Ages to do so.

Fig. 60 shows the *cantharis* or blister-beetle, which, under the name of Spanish fly, is still used in some parts of the world for medicinal or aphrodisiac purposes. In the Middle Ages it was renowned for its power as a vesicant – it could raise blisters on the skin. Here we see it enclosed in a simple rectangular frame, but most unusually it is seen against a habitat, or at least a fragment of landscape as background. This indicates a late 13th-century artist with an unusual passion for natural history, and also one who anticipated the interest in landscape which is usually thought of as beginning in the 14th century. The uncluttered ink line used to portray *cantharis* is much better adapted to rendering the structure of the insect than illumination, or ink and wash. While the picture of *cantharis* is not sufficiently accurate in its anatomy to be immediately recognisable to a modern entomologist as *lytta vesicatoria* (Spanish fly), individual parts are drawn with an attention to detail which suggests that the artist understood the function of particular organs. Probably to the bug-hunter of the day these drawings would have been quite accurate enough to identify his prey.

In the course of the 13th century a new generation of books of medicinal simples grew up alongside the Pseudo-Apuleius group, and eventually came to surpass them in popularity. The new generation built on material incorporated in translations from the Arabic, providing both new substances and different recipes. Possibly because this new material was translated, early manuscripts of the new group do not appear to have been illustrated, or at least no examples survive of illustrated manuscripts.

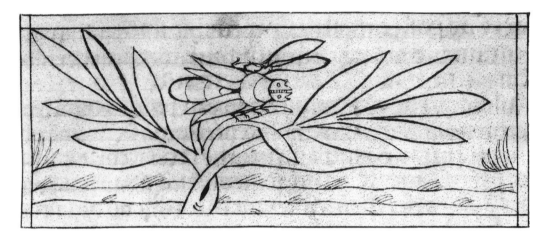

The earliest known example of an illustrated manuscript of *Tractatus de herbis* comes from the first half of the 14th century, and was made in Apulia in southern Italy. Perhaps the Italian illustrators of *Tractatus de herbis* had access to Arabic illustrated manuscripts; this was certainly the case with romances and other secular manuscripts from Campania at the same period. Whatever it was that prompted the illustration of *Tractatus de herbis* there is a clear break with the pictorial tradition of Pseudo-Apuleius. Fig. 61 shows a scene from the very first of these manuscripts known to us. It has been hailed as the first sign of a return to observation of nature in the Middle Ages, and even as the precursor of landscape painting as we know it today. Whereas Pseudo-Apuleius manuscripts show human figures dramatically struggling with rabid dogs or serpents, here we have a genre scene, with a man busy hewing sulphur or brimstone out of a volcanic landscape. In Campania such a scene would not have been unusual. The houses jumbled together are the conventional symbol for an Italian town. The stick-like man, with his flat-brimmed hat with a crown, recurs in several other scenes in this manuscript. Perspective and scale are conspicuous by their absence, and the colour is applied rather crudely, but the scene is very lively and eye-catching nonetheless. In the distance, sulphur fires can be seen. Sulphur itself was not so important a medicinal substance as 'flowers of sulphur'. This was a product of refining the raw sulphur, and it featured in a great number of medieval recipes as a laxative, a resolvent, or a sudorific (stimulating sweat).

It was also applied for cases of skin disease of different types.

Running up through the middle of the scene, with no regard to incongruity, are the stalk and flowers of a *sempervivum* or houseleek. Despite the flatness of this painting, with a uniform green wash over the leaves, the illustration does in fact succeed in capturing the pinky-orange flower and the close rosette of leaves near the root. There is a distinct lack of proportion in the long thin stem of the houseleek, and close attention to detail goes hand in hand with a cavalier disregard for design in the composition as a whole. But still the overall effect is much closer to observation from nature than any of the later Pseudo-Apuleius manuscripts. The houseleek would have been very easy to observe, as it grew on the walls and roofs of houses. Despite the occasional inclusion of details observed in living plants, however, we are still a long way yet from the individualised plant portrait, for which we have to wait until the end of the 14th century.

This next milestone is reached in the famous herbal written for Francesco Carrara II, Lord of Padua, by a Paduan monk named Jacopo Filippo, about 1400. Francesco Carrara II made his court at Padua a centre of scientific and literary pursuits; unfortunately his patronage was short-lived, since the Venetians arrested him, and had him strangled in a Venetian gaol in 1406. The herbal is an Italian translation of an Arabic work by Serapion the Younger, and though less than half of the intended illustration was ever completed, the manuscript is famous internationally for its faithfulness to observed detail and its beautiful colouring. Fig. 62 shows a melon, painted in gouache. The finely gradated colours, the detail of the veining, the use of highlights, the irregular outline of the leaves, the different sizes and stages of development of the fruit, all conspire to tell us that this painting was based on close observation of one particular specimen of the plant. There is no suspicion here of a formal pattern, though the way the root and main stem are portrayed upright rather belies the creeping nature of the plant. Probably the artist simply wanted to achieve the most effective pre-

Fig. 61
This illustration of a figure in a sulphurous landscape belongs to the first manuscript herbal in the West which shows a recognisably modern interest in landscape, as well as the first signs of a return to naturalism in depicting plants. The plant is the common houseleek.
BL, Egerton MS 747, f. 88v

Fig. 62
A plant portrait, depicting melons, from the herbal made for Francesco Carrara II, Lord of Padua, c. 1400. Naturalism in Western manuscript painting here reaches its apogee.

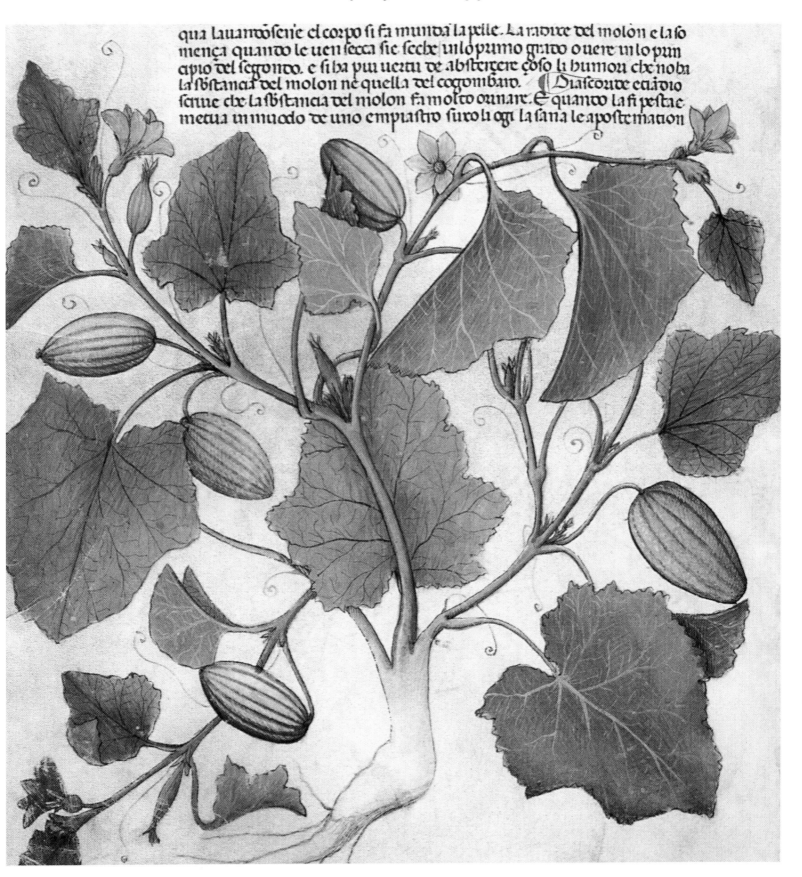

Fig. 63
A westernised vision of the famous balsam garden of Old Cairo (Fustat), showing the seven pools of water, and the jars to catch the balsam. From a manuscript illustrated in Lombardy, c. 1400. *BL, Sloane MS 4016, f. 10v*

tradition of the Arabic medical *tacuina* or handbooks, reducing the characteristics of different plants to a series of complexions and virtues which have their origin in the physiology of the four humours. This chapter on the melon begins 'Galen writes . . .', and describes the melon as being cold and wet in the second degree by complexion; its primary virtue is to disperse the viscous humour which congregates in many different parts of the body. Several recipes which use melon prepared in different ways, and in various combinations with other substances, follow after the physiological analysis. The new spirit of plant illustration, with its bias towards aesthetic rather than utilitarian values, makes an odd partner for the abstract medical terminology and recipes of the text.

The new books of medicinal simples also gave the illustrator a chance to indulge his passion for mythological or romance-based subjects. Balsam, the aromatic resin obtained from the balsam fir, gave the illustrator of Fig.63 an excellent opportunity to use a theme borrowed from the medieval romances of Alexander the Great. The balsam tree grows in the middle of a walled garden, which contains seven pools of water and four standing jars, with a couple of soldiers outside to guard it. All these elements – the walled garden, the jars to catch balsam, and the seven fountains – are first found in an early 14th century frontispiece to the Alexander story. The Alexander illustrations recall, in their turn, travellers' tales of the actual balsam garden of 'Babylon' or Old Cairo in Egypt, where there were both fountains and jars to catch balsam resin. The caption at the top of the page gives a transliteration of Arabic words for balsam, and in the whole illustration we can see the reflection of Islamic influence, not only on Western *materia medica*, but on Western art too. Of course the wall and the soldiers have been given a superficially Western appearance, but the theme is definitely oriental.

sentation possible on the flat page. Though there is no clear indication of perspective or spatial depth, the way in which the illustration overflows into the margin (it is cut off too at the page edges) reminds us that we are dealing with a three-dimensional object, not just a design which echoes the two-dimensionality of the script.

Whether this individualised plant portrait is in fact a better guide to plant recognition than something more generalised and schematic, is another question. Here the modern technique of plant portraiture based on minute observation is more in evidence than concern for plant recognition. The text on the other hand is very much in line with the

This particular manuscript seems to have been illustrated in Lombardy around 1400, and is remarkable for leaving out almost all of the medical information, save a few synonyms for different substances. The text has become entirely secondary in importance to

Mel.

Nature c 7f m:° melioz cc co. qð cst in sauo .uiuamētii. mirðificat la
rat 7 pbibet cozuptioē; carniū 7 alioz humectat .nocumētis. sitim effi
cit 7 ouertitur remotio nocumtcī pomis mucis.

Fig. 64
Mel or honey —
a very common
ingredient in medieval
medicines. From
the *Theatrum sanitatis,*
c. 1400.
Rome,
Biblioteca Casanatense,
MS 4182, tav. 181

Fig. 65
An apothecary's shop.
The apothecary is very
likely also a physician,
to judge from his dress.
The round object on
a hook is a flat dish
used for mixing
ingredients,
and apothecary jars
and boxes stand
on the shelves behind.
From a French
early 14th-century
manuscript.
BL, Sloane MS 1977,
f. 49v

the illustration, and the illustrator is at least as interested in the entertainment value of his pictures as in practical matters – such as identifying plants. These later representatives of the manuscript tradition tended to contain more and more medicinal simples, with an ever-growing proportion of exotics, which in turn gave the illustrator more room to introduce new imagery from all kinds of different sources (see Fig. 64).

Up to this point we have been talking about medicinal simples – that is to say those substances with a medicinal action, but as yet uncompounded with others. However, most of the medicines used in the Middle Ages were of course compounded – by mixing together various simples and sometimes subjecting them to chemical processes. Many of the resulting concoctions were incredibly complicated, with dozens of ingredients, many of them exotic. One which crops up in hundreds of manuscripts is the legendary 'mithridate', supposed to have been invented by Mithridates V, King of Pontus, as an antidote to all known poisons. Its ingredients would have been very expensive and difficult to assemble, so it is not surprising that mithridate was regarded as an electuary (or paste) reserved for kings alone. Most compounds, whether in the form of pastes, potions, or ointments, were less complicated, but needed some professional expertise to make. A great many physicians combined their strictly medical role with that of apothecary, and dispensed their own compound medicines.

The apothecary's shop where compound medicines could be bought over the counter must have been a familiar sight in every town. Such a shop is the subject of Fig. 65, which comes from a French manuscript of the early 14th century. The shop here seems to have been built into a highly stylised two-dimensional picture of a walled medieval town. The physician-apothecary, seated on a rather grand chair, appears to be lecturing to the attendant monk about an ointment in the jar he holds in his hand. Two rows of these jars are on display shelves. Decorated apothecary jars of this type are very common in medical manuscripts, even when the subject is not obviously pharmaceutical. They must have been a common

sight on open shop fronts, or on shelves in houses. The circular-shaped object hanging from a hook is a flattened depiction of a bowl, probably used for mixing simples. This illustration is the frontispiece to *Circa instans*, an alphabetical book of medicinal ingredients compiled at Salerno in the 12th century; it shows us how the prescriptions listed in the text would be transformed into the medicines which the patient bought over the counter.

Some drawings in a 15th-century English manuscript give us an overview of the whole process of medicine preparation, from the gathering of the ingredients to the mixing of compound drugs. Fig. 66 shows two rows of pictures, with captions to them running above. They are scenes from a potted history of medicine which begins with Apollo, its supposed founder (see Fig. 94). Apollo passed on his skills to Aesculapius, his son, and Aesculapius

Fig. 66
Aesculapius and Asclepius, supposedly the son and grandson of Apollo, are instructing others in the collection, preparation, and dispensation of medicines. Hippocrates (or Galen) is holding up a jordan to the sun; he should be 'shewing certain qualities in refyning', according to this 15th-century manuscript.
BL, Sloane MS 6, f. 175v

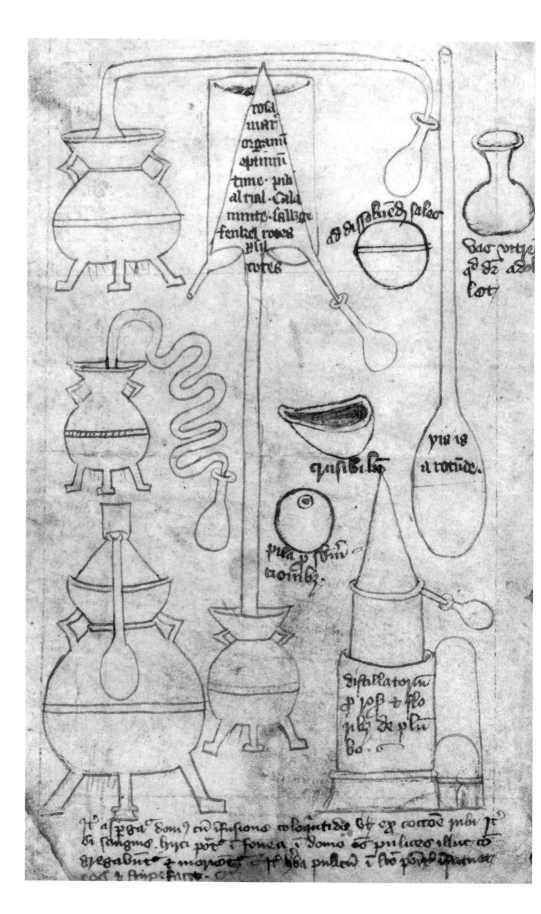

Fig. 67
The furnaces, stills, and other apparatus shown were used for the alchemical transmutation of metals, but also for preparing medicines, notably alcohol and infusions of herbs. From a 15th-century English manuscript.
BL, Sloane MS 3548, f. 25

in turn passed them on to Asclepius, his son. But unfortunately at this point in the medical succession Aesculapius and Asclepius were slain by thunderbolts for healing a man whom God wished to die. (It is worth noting that this story has made two distinct characters out of the son of Apollo who was slain by Zeus for bringing Hippolytus back to life.) For 300 years after this no man dared study or practise physic for fear of suffering the same fate.

On the upper left of our picture sits Aesculapius, wearing a resplendent head-dress; he is seen handing over a bowl of medicine to a patient. Aesculapius is supposed to have healed by means of pharmacy and medicine, according to the caption. Next to this scene, three men, under instruction from 'Aschepius' (Asclepius), are gathering roots, herbs, flowers and fruit into baskets. At below left, Asclepius is demonstrating the use of a balance in pharmacy, while, under his supervision, others make powders, confections, and electuaries (medicinal pastes), with the help of a mortar and pestle. Various herbs and simples are scattered on the table, which is finely decorated with a cup motif and inlay patterns.

The story goes on to relate that Ypocras (Hippocrates) revived the art of medicine after a 300-year gap. His work was clarified and augmented by Galen. The caption over the last scene tells us that Ypocras and Galen are showing certain quantities used in refining. But although the array of cups and boxes on the table certainly suggests that Ypocras (or Galen) is demonstrating how simples can be refined into new medicinal products, the sage actually seems to be holding a urine glass up to the sun for diagnosis (the basket for carrying the jordan is under the table).

Whatever it is that the medical authorities are up to in these scenes, we do get a good idea of the baskets, scales, bowls, cups, boxes, and mortar and pestle which would have passed for standard apothecary's equipment in the business of gathering, measuring, and processing medicines. The draughtsman combines an eye for fine detail with the figure and drapery style of the much admired

Flemish school of his period. The costumes of the assistants, with their jackets to the knees and small stand-up collars, are clearly contemporary, and suggest a date for the manuscript of the second decade of the 15th century.

The refining process supposed to have been introduced by Ypocras and Galen was just one of a number of medical applications of the branch of the mechanical arts known as alchemy. The main object of alchemy, as practised in the West, was the transmutation of metals in general, and the making of gold in particular. However, some of the techniques used could also help in the production of medicines. Applied to vegetable simples, for example, distillation gave rise to a number of aromatic substances, oils, and medicinal waters (rosewater and melissa cordial, for instance). Applied to compounds which contained salt, sal ammoniac, sulphur, vitriol, or saltpetre, in various combinations, it produced *aquae acutae* (sharp waters), ancestors of our hydrochloric, sulphuric, and nitric acids. Applied to wine, it produced an *aqua ardens* (burning water) or alcohol, for which recipes first appeared in the 12th century. Alcohol in particular came to play an ever larger role in the preparation of medicines, and was extensively used for anaesthetic and pain killing purposes. Nevertheless, these achievements must have been considered insignificant by the alchemists themselves, who set themselves the target of producing nothing less than the elixir of life.

Fig. 67 shows a page devoted to pictures of alchemical apparatus, with some labels in a mixture of Latin and English. It comes from a collection of medical treatises of the 15th century, English in origin. On the other side of the leaf is a diagram of urine glasses with the usual captions explaining the different significations of colour (see p. 46). This single leaf is not paper – like the rest of the book – but parchment. Probably it was incorporated in the book during the 15th century, and it fits in quite nicely with the surrounding text which describes several complicated medicinal recipes involving the boiling up of a mixture of herbs in a cauldron.

Four of the pieces of apparatus shown on this leaf have been added after the others (they are slightly darker in outline, and are all captioned). Within the arrow shape at the top centre are recorded the names of a variety of root-herbs (rosemary, thyme, calamint, sage, fennel, persil, and origanum), and at the bottom right the 'distillatory' is said to be for roses and flowers from the cauldron. The numerous jars for drawing off liquids from the larger apparatus are receivers to catch infusions of these herbs. Another process mentioned is the dissolving of salts, in the globe at the upper right. The larger pieces of apparatus are furnaces and stills used in the staple processes of distillation and sublimation (conversion of solids into vapour). Alchemists were interested in separating and conjoining the four elements as part of their art, so alchemy and medicine had a lot of theoretical concepts in common too.

At the foot of this page of illustrations of alchemical apparatus, the scribe has written out a prescription of goat's blood. If placed in a hole within the house, he says, it attracts fleas, who succumb upon drinking it. An invaluable household tip, with no elaborate equipment needed.

CAUTERY AND SURGERY

Fig. 68
Hippocrates presides
over scenes of cautery
applied to different
ailments. From
a manuscript of the
Chirurgia of Rolando
da Parma, c.1300.
Rome,
Biblioteca Casanatense,
MS 1382, f. 19

Surgery offers plenty of scope for visual drama, and it was this drama that appealed to the medieval artist. Where today we would use film, the medieval artist had to make do with a sequence of still images; but while his resources were different, his aim was often the same – to tell a story. Plenty of pathos, and life-or-death tension, can be extracted from scenes of surgery, laced with moments of brutal comedy. There were limitations of course, and not just to do with the use of stills rather than moving film – the medieval artist was normally illustrating a particular text, and one that was factual instead of fictional. But the opportunity offered by the surgeon, his instruments, and his patient, was too good for the artist to miss, and scenes of surgical practice are one of the commoner sorts of secular illustration in medieval manuscripts. This type of surgical illustration, which concentrated on the visual drama of the subject, was destined in the end to pass away with the manuscript book. In the later 16th century, the technical resources of woodcut and engraving were geared to the multiplication of pictures which would help readers of the printed book to understand techniques of surgery, or to show up details of anatomy. But enough of the older sort of surgery illustration has survived for us to appreciate what has been lost.

We have spoken of the end of medieval surgery illustration, but not the beginning. In the beginning, before there were pictures of surgery, there were pictures of cautery. The earliest images of operations which have come down to us in manuscript books are of cautery, and date from the 9th century AD. These are pictures which show the appropriate points at which the hot iron should be applied to the body as a remedy against specific illnesses. Cautery at that time had more perhaps in common with modern acupuncture than with the use today of cautery techniques in microsurgery applications (sealing the end of a particular blood vessel, for instance). Although what has come down to us in the form of pictures and a few short captions does not tell us much about the theory behind cautery, they do reveal a complex set of ideas on the ways in which the balance of the humours in the body can be manipulated by deliberate intervention.

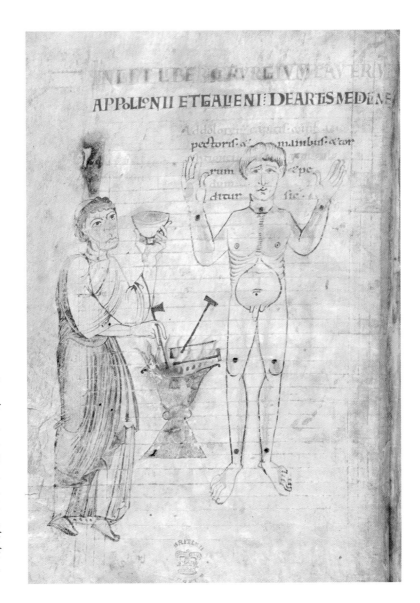

When any one of the four humours predominates at the expense of the others, it can cause disease – the type varies according to the particular circumstances of the patient. Cautery is seen as one means of attempting to readjust the balance of the humours, by drawing off 'sick' or excessive humours through the ulcer caused by cautery application. These ideas were in currency in the medical schools of Alexandria in the 2nd century AD. We may assume that in this late Alexandrian period atlases of the points at which the cautery instrument was to be applied were already in existence, and that the first illustrations that have survived are descendants of these early diagrams. By the time they reached the medieval illustrator the cautery pictures had lost all traces of any complete text they may have been intended to illustrate, and were accompanied only by the briefest of instructions: for example, 'for eyes, and for stopping them running, measure three

inches in from both ears and burn with a broad cautery' (see Fig. 68).

Fig. 69 comes from a manuscript, quite probably of English origin, which dates from about 1100. It is the first page of a series of four, showing cautery figures in various postures. The physician stands on the left offering a beaker to the patient, who is marked with black spots representing cautery points at the neck, wrists, knees, and ankles. Between the two men there is a brazier in which different types of cautery instrument are being heated. The long robes and cap of the physician strongly suggest a Byzantine original, and many of the faces in the whole series indicate that the artist was used to the conventions of sacred art. The composition here is outlined in a brown ink, brushed over with washes of sepia, orange, and green.

Running above the picture is a title, or rather

ad cenelicu et dipsnicæ incendut sic.

Fig. 70

Cautery applied to the patient's
chest for respiratory problems.
An assistant passes a red-hot iron
to the physician, who holds a cup.

*Florence, Biblioteca Laurenziana,
MS Plut. 73.41, f. 122*

incipit (opening words), for the book as it
must once have been. It reads, in translation
'Here begins the book of surgery and cautery
of Apollonius and Galen: the art of medicine'. Very probably the author of this incipit was simply trying to impress the reader with
mention of two authorities, Apollonius (but
which one?), and Galen, the greatest medical
author of them all. After such an impressive
beginning, the fragments of text left make a
poor show. The caption round the head of
the patient reads, in translation: 'for sickness
of the head and swelling of the chest, and tor-
turing pain of hands, knees, and feet, burn
thus'. This is not what we would call a description of a specific disease, and the terms used
are equally vague throughout.

The posture of the patient, facing directly
out from the page, with his arms upraised,
make it likely that this part of the picture at
least is derived from a schematic atlas of the
human body rather than a naturalistic figure.
The fact that he is portrayed entirely naked,
although undoubtedly it makes the purpose
of the picture easier to understand, may also
indicate that the picture has its origins in a
classical precursor. The medieval artist tended to use nudity only in places where the text
demanded it. The cup or beaker, by contrast,
is of symbolic significance. It occurs in other pictures, not in the doctor's hand, as here,
but alongside the patient, and stands for the
use of a soporific or pain killing drug, given
in the form of a drink. Recipes for such drinks
are found in several of these early medieval
texts. The message conveyed is that before
applying the cautery to the places indicated,
the doctor should first administer one of these
potions.

Reconstructing the gradual build-up of the
different elements in this picture, we might
start from the hypothesis that there had originally been in Alexandrian times a series of
schematic drawings of the human body, used
to show where the cautery should be applied.
The figures of the physicians had possibly
entered the series later, added by Byzantine
artists; they give it a more naturalistic flavour.
The symbolic cups or beakers too were probably later additions, from what we know of the
fondness of the medieval artist for such devices.

If this cautery series has a long history, there are three pictures of surgical operations which may be as old – though far fewer of these sets are known, and the earliest dates from the 12th century. By a quirk of fate, two of the four sets known are to be found in the British Library. Each set contains three pictures, and both the British Library versions are intriguing enough to be worth showing here (see Figs. 71-73) The three surgical operations – couching of cataract, extirpation of nasal polyps, and excision of haemorrhoids – have survived together as a unit, but they are sometimes also found after the cautery series we have just considered. Why these three operations, and these three alone, should have come down to us from the 12th century is not clear. They do represent the sort of operations which a conservative surgeon of the time might have risked, without too much danger to the patient and with a fair chance of success, given the resources available. But we should beware of supposing too readily that these pictures must have been created in order to instruct the surgeon in the performance of these three operations. As was suggested in Chapter I, some pictures were copied simply as a means of preserving images sanctioned by the authority of a long tradition. The surgery operations may fall into this category (see p. 18).

The earlier of the two manuscripts is Harley MS 1585, which comes from the region of the valley of the Meuse, and is mid 12th century in date. The illustration in Fig. 71 is of the extirpation of a nasal polyps; it is on the bottom half of a page which has a depiction of the couching of cataract at the top. There is a caption above the illustration which reads, 'growth in the nose should be cut out thus'. The curious posture of the physician here is probably the result of the artist not understanding his model: somewhere along the line the bench on which he must once have been sitting has been lost. The same scene in the other British Library manuscript also shows the physician sitting on nothing at all. The physician holds a knife specially shaped to allow insertion into the nostril, where it is used for cutting away the growth. In his left hand he holds a pipe, used for blowing down a special kind of dust after the operation; it

Fig. 71
Extirpation of a nasal polyps. The surgeon holds a knife in one hand, and a pipe through which to blow a healing powder, in the other. The patient holds a bowl to catch the blood. From a mid 12th century manuscript.
BL, Harley MS 1585, f. 9v

was supposed to have healing properties. The patient holds a bowl to catch the l lood. Sensibly enough, the artist has exaggerated the length of his nose in order to make the point of the scene clearer. The fact that the figures are drawn in outline also makes for clarity – although, as in other pictures in the same manuscript, this picture was intended to be washed with colour.

With the second of the two manuscripts, the colour was certainly not forgotten, as can be seen from Fig.72. The physician is holding in his right hand a tapering needle-like instrument, which he applies to the patient's eye. We are left in no doubt that the patient suffers from cataract, because he is not given a normal pupil in either eye, but just a slit. The patient holds an ointment box in his hands, which may be a symbolic reminder of the need for post operative medication. The caption over the figures' heads reads: 'the whitish liquid of the eyes should be cut away thus'. The 'whitish liquid' is a reference to the ancient theory that cataracts were formed by a whitish liquid descending from the brain. But there remains a little doubt as to whether

Fig. 72
Cataracts were supposed to be formed by a whitish liquid running down from the brain. Here the surgeon uses a needle to move the cataract off the eye (or perhaps, as the caption suggests, he is cutting it out). The patient holds an ointment jar. From a late 12th century manuscript. *BL, Sloane MS 1975, f. 93*

Albule oculorum sic excu cuciuntur.

the surgeon was supposed to push the cataract to the corner of the eye with his needle, or to cut it out, as the caption seems to suggest.

The last of the three operations we shall consider is that for the excision of haemorrhoids. To judge from the frequency and length with which procedures for dealing with this uncomfortable ailment are dealt with in surgical texts of the Middle Ages, this operation must have often been called for. Certainly the guidance offered by one picture (Fig. 73) is specific on several points. The surgeon operates with a clawed separator in his left hand, and a business-like knife in his right. The patient adopts an appropriate position for the operation. But the picture is still puzzling in several respects. Presumably the patient stands over a bowl to catch the copious flow of blood to be expected. However the blood in this picture is plainly missing the bowl (it can be seen at the surgeon's left knee). What is the curious oblong object on which the patient does not quite seem to be leaning? Note too the unnatural articulation of the patient's head and shoulders – it looks almost as if a human head had been stuck on the body of some four-legged animal.

The answer again seems to be that the artist was working not from a mind's eye picture of the operation, nor even an appreciation of physical possibilities, but from an imperfectly understood, yet faithfully copied, model. In any case our artist makes no effort to turn his picture into a single intelligible image. The cruciform decoration on the oblong object was perhaps added as a semi-ecclesiastical motif with which the artist was familiar, to give significance to what was to him a meaningless part of the model before him. In Harley MS 1585 it is left unadorned as a plain rectangle. Perhaps originally it had been some table or bench on which the patient leaned for support, or perhaps it was a brazier – like those which occur in the neighbouring cautery illustrations. Our conclusion must be that the artists of these early series of surgical operations were far more concerned to transmit to posterity the images they found in manuscripts older still, than to convey any practical information about the details of surgical technique.

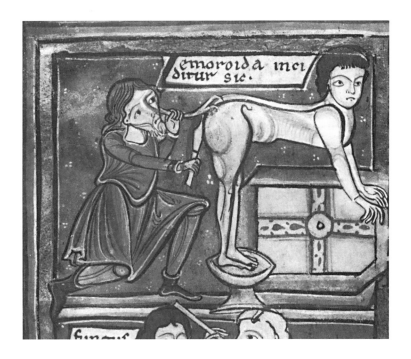

Both these manuscripts were written in, and probably owned by, monastic houses. These would have had infirmaries, in which the monks them selves – and perhaps strangers too – underwent surgical operations. Documentary evidence suggests that the ordinary run of minor surgery was in the hands of *medici manuales*, medical auxiliaries who were usually laymen in the employ of the monastery, and who would have served as barbers and bloodletters too. Such activities could be regarded as not entirely fitting for the monks themselves, though they were not forbidden the shedding of blood (see p. 26). But the three operations pictured in these manuscripts would more likely have fallen in any case to the lot of someone with training in surgery. Warin, twentieth Abbot of St Albans (d.1195), received such a training at Salerno – as his successor, John of Cella, did at Paris – and only men of this stature would have been regarded as competent to perform this sort of surgery.

Outside the monastery too, there were surgeons. The records and references in chronicles which have come down to us from the early Middle Ages are scanty, but we can assume the existence of secular physicians who might have practised surgery. Some few

would have been attached to courts and important noblemen; many more were probably itinerant cutters for the stone, or eye doctors, herniotomists, or teeth-pullers and barbers with a side-line in minor surgery. These men were most unlikely to own books (luxury items then), or have access to such pictures as we have seen. Their lore was probably passed down from master to pupil, or father to son; even when surgery was instituted as a part of the curriculum at Salerno in the 12th century, what was learnt from texts never replaced the practical necessity of apprenticeship, and learning by watching a thing done.

After the 12th-century series of cautery and surgery pictures, there is a sudden hiatus in the production of such illustrations; very few pictures of surgical procedures can be dated to the first three-quarters of the 13th century. There are several possible explanations for this break. In the late 12th and early 13th centuries we know that there was a rapid increase in the production of new surgical texts – not new in the sense of containing a wealth of new ideas or procedures, but in the sense of the construction of coherent textbooks rather than the transmission of ancient fragments. The authors relied very much on what they could learn from these fragments, and from the new translations into Latin from Arabic of the 11th and 12th centuries. This last was the main, if circuitous, route by which the ancient Greek medical authors reached the West. They also relied to some extent on their own experience, as occasional anecdotes or case-histories tell us. But the new authors knitted all their different sources into continuous prose in an ordered sequence proceeding from head to foot, in a way that could be used by teachers and pupils. This discontinuity in surgical literature may have contributed to the disappearance of the older pictorial tradition.

During the 13th century the teaching of surgery became institutionalised at Salerno, as already mentioned, at Bologna, and at other north Italian schools. Frederick II of Hohenstaufen's regulations for Salerno in 1231 required the study of surgery as part of the training of a physician, and also stipulated a

Fig. 74
Reduction of dislocation of the vertebrae with the use of a pulley. From an 11th-century Byzantine manuscript of the commentary of Apollonius of Citium on the *De articulis* of Hippocrates. These illustrations were not discovered in the West until the 15th century.
Florence, Biblioteca Laurenziana, MS Plut. 74.7, f. 200

Fig. 75
Compound fracture
of the skull. Six scenes
showing progressive
stages in the operation
described by Roger
Frugardi of Parma.
On the top register are
the first three scenes
from a life of Christ.
From an early
14th-century
manuscript
from France.
*BL, Sloane MS 1977,
f. 2*

separate licence for practising surgeons. So the great scholastic era of the 13th century embraced medicine and surgery as well as philosophy, theology, and law, and it had the new texts to work with. But the university schools were not places in which surgical illustration seems to have flourished, despite what to us seems its obvious potential as a teaching aid; scholastic method favoured verbal forms of teaching rather than visual (see p. 18).

So the gap which separates the older images, going as far back perhaps as Alexandria, from the new illustrations of the late 13th and early 14th centuries, may have to do with the writing of the new texts and the university environment. Why though were the new texts finally given illustrations at the later date? After all, the first of the new textbooks, the *Chirurgia* of Roger Frugardi of Parma, was written about 1180, but – as far as we know – was first illustrated about a century later. This phenomenon seems to have occurred at the same time in relation to medical books in general, and, for that matter, secular illustration of all types. As we saw in Chapter I, the mass production (in manuscript terms anyway) of romances and histories, the use of the French language, and the opening up of a new market for illuminated manuscripts amongst laymen, were all important factors in stimulating secular illustration. Surgery books benefited from these conditions too.

The finest single illustrated surgical book of the Middle Ages, based on the French text of Roger Frugardi and executed probably near Amiens, dates from the first decade of the 14th century. It is now in the British Library, and illustrated here (Figs. 75, 76, 78). Its sinuous dancing figures, rich colours, and resemblance to a strip-cartoon remind us of the romances and histories which must have come from the same workshop. But it also shows remarkable fidelity to the instructions of the text, and suggests a far greater acquaintance with the realities of contemporary surgery than did the early form of surgical illustration.

As may be seen from Fig.75, this manuscript has another striking feature, which distinguishes it from all other surgical illustra-

tion. The top register of the three on the page is devoted to the beginning of the story of Christ's life, while the lower two registers proceed with the head-to-toe development of the surgery theme. This conjunction of sacred art with secular, as well as being unprecedented, is also without, as yet, any satisfactory explanation. It might seem at first sight that in such a religious age matters of the body, like medicine and surgery, would as likely as not be interspersed with references to the spirit, or the scriptures. But in fact this was not the case. Sacred and profane were kept in separate compartments, and it is all the more surprising that they should be conjoined in the design of the page as here. No sort of parallelism between the head-to-toe surgery series and the life of Christ seems to be present. The seventeen-page block of illustrations was placed in the manuscript before the beginning of the Roger Frugardi text (which of course has no relevance to the life of Christ). The life of Christ series was more in line with the normal output of an illuminating workshop than the surgery illustrations; it certainly adds a richer ingredient to the overall design of the page, and perhaps was superimposed on purely aesthetic grounds, at the request of the (unknown) customer who bought the manuscript.

The sequence of surgical illustrations follows, with some curious exceptions, the order of the French text of Roger Frugardi. But the fact that the illustrations are physically separate from the text means that it would have been very difficult, if not impossible, to use the illustrations as a visual aid to the understanding of the text. It is sometimes hard in any case to establish a direct relationship between the individual picture and the point in the text to which it relates, and generally it becomes harder as the sequence progresses.

The first full page of six surgery illustrations (Fig. 75) is the easiest to follow with an eye on the text. Reading from top to bottom and from left to right, the whole series of six forms one operation, that for a compound fracture of the skull. First the surgeon investigates with his spatula-shaped probe. Then he extracts bone splinters by means of a pair

of tweezers with cupped grips. In the third scene, again with the help of the probe, he places a piece of linen between the *dura mater* (a hard membrane covering the brain) and the skull, in order to protect the brain. On the bottom register, we see the surgeon putting a protective bandage under the scalp in order to soak up pus, and prevent it getting to the membrane. Then he cleans up the wound with a marine sponge. Here in fact there is a divergence between author and illustrator, since the text specifically requires a dry sponge, whereas the surgeon carries a bowl into which the sponge is presumably dipped. In the last of the six scenes, the surgeon dresses the wound with linen soaked in egg-white, again with the help of the spatula-shaped probe.

There are very few miniatures or drawings from the Middle Ages which tell the story of an operation from start to finish, and indeed this first page is the only such sequence in this manuscript. The remaining miniatures can best be construed as snapshots of a particular stage in one of the operations described by Roger Frugardi. It is not surprising that the one complete sequence should be for treatment of a fractured skull, for this kind of operation was the tour de force of the medieval surgeon. This was not the kind of thing an itinerant operator would undertake, but only the university-trained practitioner. The surgeon in this manuscript is plainly of the latter sort, since he wears the long robe of a *magister*. It is worth noting that there are no symbolic cups of anaesthetic in evidence, or sponges soaked in soporific preparations. But in the second (and potentially most painful) scene of our sequence, the removal of the bone splinters, the surgeon does have his foot firmly on that of the patient, suggesting that this was accepted surgical practice (although not described in the text).

However, there is an element of stylisation in this manuscript which should warn us against taking specific details as authoritative guides to surgical technique. Throughout, the poses of surgeon and patient reflect the characteristics of the high gothic style favoured in French miniatures of the period. They seem often to be engaged in a swaying dance, on which the viewer's attention is focused because

Fig. 76
Reducing a dislocated shoulder. This ancient
procedure requires the surgeon to pull down
the patient's arm. Medical technique is better served
by the artist than perspective — see the table legs.
From a French early 14th-century manuscript.
BL, Sloane MS 1977, f. 6

Fig. 77
Rolando reduces
a dislocated jaw using
his feet for leverage.
A north Italian
manuscript of the
Chirurgia of Rolando
da Parma, c.1300.
Although very different
in style to the Roger
Frugardi illustrations,
this series shares many
of the same surgical
subjects.
*Rome,
Biblioteca Casanatense,
MS 1382, f. 19*

of the lack of background distractions. The
gesture of the arms with palms of the hands
held out horizontally is particularly characteristic, even when in real life the patient
would find such gestures impossible. The faces
are always impassive, whatever is being done.
Overall the effect is of a dainty dance of surgeon and patient, all the more striking because
in most other contemporary forms of figure
composition the scene is cluttered with bodies and objects. Here only the basic tools prescribed by the text are present, with an occasional line of ointment jars on a shelf to suggest a context. Otherwise the hypnotic rhythm
established by the two protagonists holds
sway.

Another single frame from the same manuscript, but for once involving more than two
figures, shows the procedure for reducing a
dislocated shoulder (Fig. 76). The surgeon,
holding the patient's left foot with one hand,

pulls down on his left arm with the other.
The patient's shoulder is supported by a pole
with a padded bole at the centre, which the
two assistants hold at each end. The small
table on which the patient stands seems to
have three legs, but all at one side, showing
a fine disregard for physical propriety. This
same procedure, as described by Roger, is
found in the ancient Hippocratic writings,
and a number of Arabic and Western manuscripts show the operation in very similar
terms. Some of the bandaging techniques
used in our manuscript also resemble earlier
illustrations, though there is not enough evidence to suggest a connection with any surviving manuscript. The unique design of this
manuscript, and the fact that so many of its
scenes have no surviving parallels, argue on
the other hand that the composition of the
pictures was the work of the master of the
workshop, and not based directly on an earlier model.

Fig. 78 shows the suturing of a lateral wound of the thorax. This particular illustration is remarkable in that the wound has been enlarged to let us see more clearly what the correct procedure is. The surgeon passes the needle through the lower, then the upper, lips of the wound, holding the lips firmly with the fingers of his other hand. This picture gives us more than the text alone supplies, and indicates that the artist must have had a pretty good idea of the basics of surgical technique. While the picture could hardly be said to be realistic – given the exaggerated size of the wound, the patient's apparent indifference, and the extra-long arms of the surgeon – it nevertheless achieves a very high level of clarity as a guide to technique.

There are plenty of other scenes in this manuscript, however, which seem to show no concern for surgical technique at all. Sometimes the patient is portrayed simply pointing to a wound, while the surgeon stands by. Sometimes it is not clear what the disease or injury is, since both parties are simply gesturing at one another. One scene shows an unconcerned patient with his tunic open to reveal a javelin and an arrow transfixing his chest! This is to illustrate the section on extracting barbed weapons, but tells the viewer nothing about how the tricky task should be performed. So the illustrations veer between graphic demonstrations of technique and scenes which are more entertaining than instructive. A very independent and individual hand was at work in this charming series.

Much more typical of the run of medieval surgical illustration is the single miniature inserted as an historiated initial in surgical, or occasionally non surgical, texts. One of the most original and innovative of medieval surgical authors was William of Saliceto, who completed a treatise on surgery at Verona in 1275 which soon became a very popular text. Many of his observations were based on first-hand clinical experience, and for a surgeon of that period he showed an abnormally strong interest in anatomy and in the use of autopsy. His treatise was aimed at those he called *medici manuales*, surgeons who worked with their hands, not those merely learned. He does show a thorough acquaintance with Arab authors, though, and often uses words directly transliterated from the Arabic, where he knows no Latin equivalent.

Fig. 79 shows the initial C[auterium] from the beginning of the first chapter of Book 5 of William's treatise. Book 5 is devoted to cautery, and the first chapter has to do with the purposes of cautery, and necessary warnings about its use. The purposes he mentions

Fig. 79
An historiated initial from the first chapter of Book V of William of Saliceto's treatise on surgery, showing a patient undergoing cautery below the knee. The 'academic' background is appropriate to William's own position as a professor of surgery in the 13th century.
BL, Additional MS 17810, f. 111

Fig. 78
Suturing a wound of the thorax. The wound has been enlarged by the artist to make the technique easier to see. The surgeon is passing the needle through the lower and upper lips of a lateral wound — probably an accurate reflection of contemporary technique. From a French early 14th-century manuscript.
BL, Sloane MS 1977, f. 6v

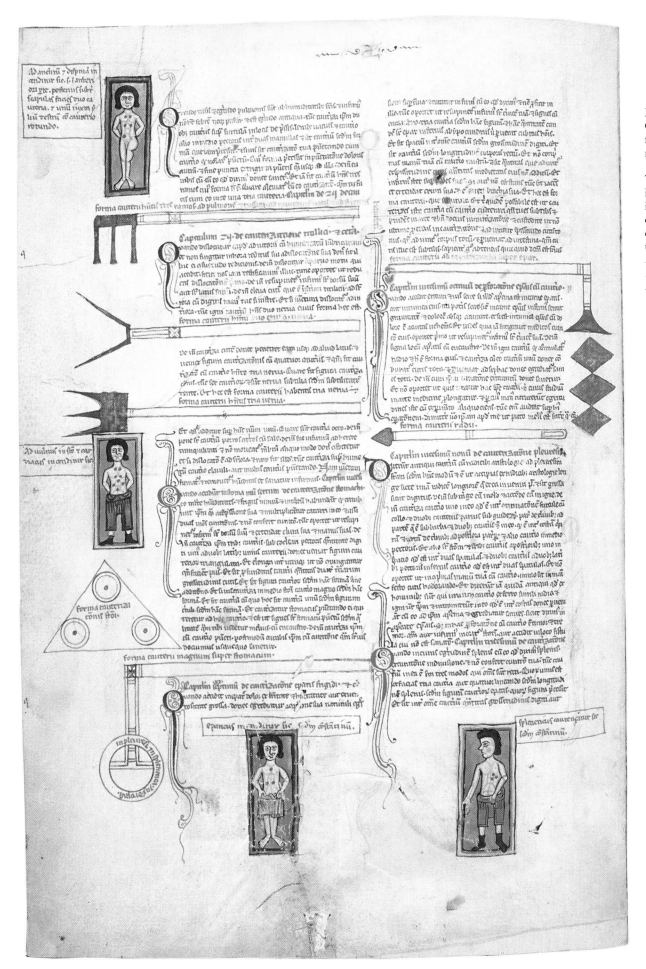

Fig. 80
Cautery instruments
from a 13th-century
manuscript of the
Chirurgia of Albucasis.
The cautery
illustrations
in manuscripts
of William of Saliceto
derive from
the Albucasis series.
*Florence,
Biblioteca Laurenziana,
MS Plut. 73.23, f. 82v*

include interference with the relative proportions of the complexions (hot, cold, moist, dry) of the human body, the expulsion of corrupt matter from a member of the body, and stanching the flow of blood. It is interesting that as a practising surgeon he is much more sceptical about the use of cautery for such general purposes as interference with the balance of the complexions than most of his predecessors and contemporaries.

The historiated initial which introduces the subject of cautery is obviously meant to indicate the scope of the book, rather than correspond to a particular passage in the text. The surgeon seems to be applying his cautery just below the patient's knee, and the end of the instrument is covered in blood. It is not at all clear, then, what this specific application of the cautery is intended to achieve. One of the most significant features of the picture is the audience gathered behind the bench on which both the surgeon and patient are sitting. The intent face of the central member of the audience suggests a gathering of medical students or apprentice surgeons, not friends and relations of the patient, or idle onlookers. William of Saliceto himself taught at Bologna, and in the university schools of medicine this kind of demonstration of surgical technique would have been an integral and essential part of the curriculum; not all university teaching relied on books or theoretical disputations. Apart from this feature, the illustration is chiefly remarkable (like the three others in the manuscript) for the quality of its composition, its fine colours, and the skilful delineation of the folds of dress.

Many William of Saliceto manuscripts, though not – as it happens – this one, contain illustrations of the cautery implements which had his seal of approval. They were usually simply outlined in the midst of a column of text. Most illustrations of surgical instruments from the Middle Ages, William's included, are derived from Arabic designs. This is not surprising, since Arabic surgical practice favoured the cautery over the knife, and they were largely responsible for promoting its widespread use in Europe. Albucasis devoted the first book of his well-known treatise 'On surgery and instruments' to the

virtues of the actual cautery (with hot iron), and illustrations to this treatise were the main channel by which Arabic designs for surgical instruments reached the West. There is a very fine Latin manuscript of the treatise, copiously illustrated, in the British Library's collections; it may be seen in Fig. 12. These abstract designs were very often misunderstood by western copyists (see p. 24). More realistic pictures of actual instruments do survive, though still on the lines established by Arabic authors.

Sloane MS 6 is a miscellany of medical texts of the early 15th century, written in English, which contains, by chance, both a translation of William of Saliceto with drawings of instruments and another set of instruments unaccompanied by text (Fig. 81). These last figures of instruments, drawn in ink, follow directly on from a series of illustrations of cupping (see Fig. 89), with which however they seem to

have no connection. The only explanation provided is the information contained in the captions to each instrument, which are in a mixture of Latin and English. These pictures were copied from a manuscript of the works of the French surgeon Guy de Chauliac. Shading and a crude use of perspective contrive to give the instruments some three dimensional solidity. For many of the instruments we have to suppose a wooden handle added, since only the iron part is shown.

The instruments shown in the left-hand column are all cauteries of different types, used to burn or sear the flesh. They are very close in design to those found in Albucasis and William of Saliceto manuscripts. Those on the third, fourth, and fifth lines down, are used in conjunction with other instruments (shown alongside) which guide the cautery and protect surrounding tissue. Similarly in the case of the *circulare* and its *plata*, shown

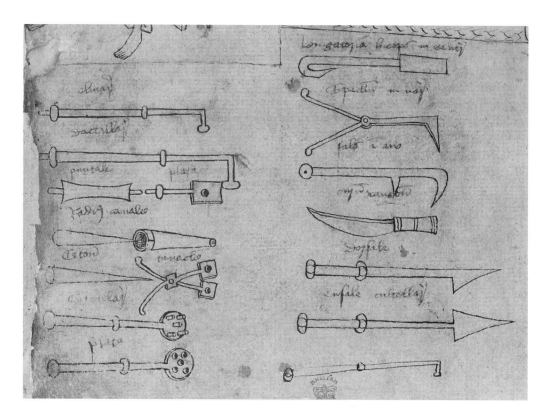

Fig. 81
A table of surgical instruments, copied from a manuscript of the works of Guy de Chauliac, a famous French surgeon of the 14th century. On the left-hand side are cauteries, on the right are an instrument for cutting out fistulae, a speculum, two more instruments for treating fistula-in-ano, and three more cauteries. From an English 15th-century manuscript. *BL, Sloane MS 6, f. 177v*

on the last two lines, the cautery is designed to make a pattern of small burns through the five circular holes.

At the top of the second column is an instrument for cutting out fistulae, in which both the hooked sharp end and the blunt end were meant to be used. The second instrument is a speculum for looking into the nostrils. The *falx* and the *curvum cavatum* below it are both instruments for use in the treatment of *fistula-in-ano*. The latter is supposed to have a groove or channel in it which will act as a director for the sharp cutting *falx*. At the bottom of the second column come three more cauteries. The last one is a button cautery which looks like the *olivare* at the top of the first column. Probably the copyist just decided to have another go at the *olivare*. (He must have copied the second column first, if he was following the order in which the instruments occur in Guy de Chauliac's text.) Unfortunately we do not know if such instruments, or ones like them, were made in accordance with the designs in this manuscript, because so few instruments have survived from the Middle Ages.

There is one set of instruments, which although we have no surviving remains of any of its members, we can be absolutely sure existed as functioning tools of the surgeon. These were the design of John of Arderne, the only English surgeon of the Middle Ages to win an international reputation. He lived in the 14th century, at a period when the Hundred Years War was giving surgery – or at least its military branch – opportunities to experiment and test techniques which it had never had before. Whether Arderne actually practised abroad as a military surgeon is a matter of some doubt, but after the Black Death in 1349 he moved from his native Newark to London, and in the 1370s wrote a number of separate treatises on general medicine and surgery. His fame rested on his skill in the performance of one particularly dangerous operation, which very few surgeons dared attempt; the treatment of *fistula-in ano* by cutting through the fistula wall. It may be that long, wet, cold, hours in the saddle, weighed down by heavy armour, contributed to this condition among the knightly class

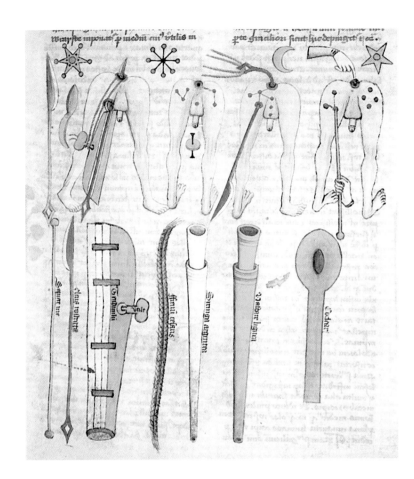

Fig. 82
The 14th-century English surgeon John of Arderne's instruments for fistula-in-ano, and diagrams showing how they were to be used. Arderne won great fame for his success in this operation. From a 15th-century manuscript.
BL, Additional MS 29301, f. 25

whom Arderne boasted as his clients. Whatever the cause, he claimed a high rate of success with his operation, which was in fact only a variant of an operation already known in antiquity. His contemporaries might have been impressed by his claims, though we may suspect that it was his conservative policy in leaving the wound fairly well alone after the operation which saved his patients.

Apart from being a successful surgeon, John of Arderne was a brilliant publicist, and his own writings, with their dramatic case-histories, personal anecdotes, and pungent style, were his best advertisement. His treatises on surgery, written originally in Latin but soon translated into English, were so constructed that a series of marginal and a few full-page illustrations formed an integral part of the text. These drawings were copied in dozens of manuscripts, and probably did more than anything else to ensure Arderne's lasting fame No doubt the copyists were encouraged in their work by the lively style of both text and

illustrations. For example, the story of how the Prince of Wales (the Black Prince) obtained his crest of an ostrich feather from blind King John of Bohemia at the battle of Crècy, was first told by Arderne, and signposted to the reader by an ostrich feather drawn in the margin of the relevant page of the manuscript.

Nearly every manuscript of Arderne's treatise *De fistula in ano* contains a full or three-quarter page illustration, which shows both the instruments Arderne recommends for the operation and the way in which each of them should be used (Fig. 82) A further device to help the reader to understand the techniques involved is the use of forms of asterisk (shown at the top of the picture), which direct him from the relevant place in the text to the corresponding illustration. So in this particular picture we have the nearest equivalent to modern illustrative technique that can be found in the Middle Ages, combining the clarity achieved by schematic diagrams, well-labelled, with a close

Fig. 83
Bandaging techniques from an 11th-century Greek manuscript of Soranus of Ephesus, *De Fasciis* (On Bandages). There are no Western equivalents to these sophisticated illustrations, even in the best surgical manuscripts. *Florence, Biblioteca Laurenziana, MS Plut. 74.7, f. 233*

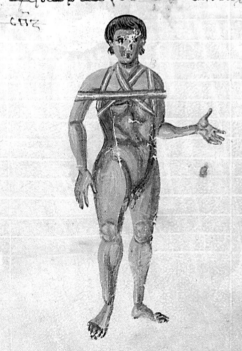

co-ordination of text and illustration. For once we can really speak with confidence of a surgical illustration obviously designed to help the reader understand, and perhaps even perform, the relevant operation.

The instrument at bottom left is a *sequere me* or 'probe', which the disembodied hand is using to investigate the sinuses in the buttock in the top right hand diagram. Next to the probe comes the *acus rostrata* or 'snouted needle', a grooved director along which the scalpel was passed. This is shown drawn through the fistula in the second diagram from the right. The third instrument (a *tendiculum*), which looks rather like something musical, did in fact have the function of tightening a ligature, as a peg does in a violin. The ligature itself is shown next on the right. Two syringes are shown next, one of silver and one of wood; Arderne particularly recommended the use of the silver syringe, though it is not shown in use here. Finally in the bottom row comes a shield or cochlear, which was probably held by the surgeon's mate to protect the rectum in the course of the operation. On the upper row there is a razor-like scalpel, and what looks to be another of the 'snouted needles'.

The basic operation was simply a division of the fistula by means of a scalpel inserted along the 'snouted needle' or director; the ligature and *tendiculum* were complications, introduced probably as a result of Arderne's reverence for Albucasis, who had described the use of such a ligature. It is perhaps a pity that the name of the greatest English medieval surgeon should be associated with an operation which seems so undignified, but Arderne deserves the credit for remarkable sophistication in the description and illustration of his operation.

The most dignified sort of surgery was undoubtedly performed on noble casualties on the battlefield. This battlefield surgery gave the surgeon an unequalled opportunity to observe the internal anatomy of the casualties – an opportunity that was far more frequent, though chancy and fleeting, than that afforded by formal dissections of corpses. Great prestige could be won too by some daring intervention in cases where caution was clearly useless. However we find very few pictures of battlefield surgery before the 16th century, when there was quite a vogue for them in connection with the new printed books of surgery.

There is one curious and very common form of illustration, which originated long before the 16th century, but whose purpose is difficult to fathom. It obviously has a bearing on battlefield wounds as well as on the operable injuries and diseases of peacetime. The wound-man is the name commonly given to this mannikin, sometimes found with anatomical figures (see Chapter 2), but just as often on its own (Fig. 84). Not all of the examples come equipped with captions like this one – a purely decorative spirit seems to have overtaken the artists of many of the most colourful examples. But this wound-man, from a 15th-century manuscript in the Wellcome Library, not only displays the weapons and sources of injury, but also comes with extensive captions and explanatory note. Amongst the weapons inflicting wounds we can see swords, clubs, arrows, a stone (on top of the head), and spear-heads. Little distinction is made between the type of wound caused, only between wounds which transfix and those which merely penetrate. There seems to be no cogent reason why any particular weapon should be associated with a wound in any particular place. Other external sources of injury are the bites of dogs, snakes, and scorpions, and thorns which impale the flesh. But some of the diseases captioned are not external injuries at all – for instance, cataract, deafness, and general paralysis. Various sorts of ulcerous sores and rashes are also illustrated.

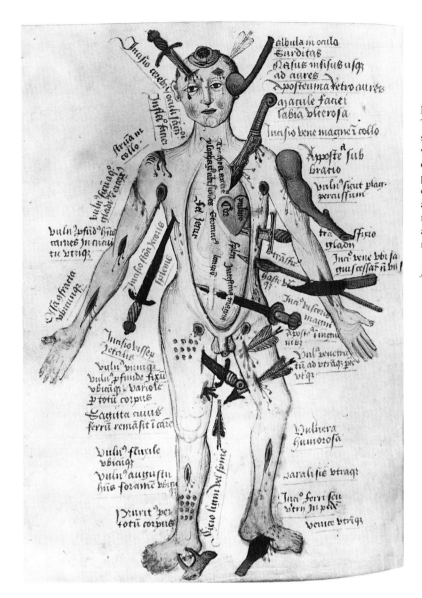

Fig. 84
The wound-man shown displaying weapons, sources of injuries, and sores, perhaps with the object of prompting the aspiring surgeon's memory. From a 15th-century manuscript. *Wellcome MS 290, f. 53v*

As an anatomical design the figure has some odd features. He stands in the usual 'arms akimbo' pose of such figures, but he has a long cavity through thorax and abdomen which looks as though it ought to contain a picture of the internal organs. A conventional heart shape is represented on the outside of the body, divided into two halves, labelled 'heart' and 'lung'. Other captions on the body show where the artist meant us to imagine a particular organ sited – oesophagus, stomach, spleen, and large intestine, for example. But no attempt is made to link them systematically with diseases or injuries.

The most likely function of a scheme like this is a teaching one. The pictures of weapons were perhaps meant simply as a reminder of some list of different types of wound and their treatment; the actual site of the injury made by a particular weapon would be an artistic convention, not a medical one. But the internal organs were surely meant to be in their correct places, if any worthwhile information was to be conveyed, and the other forms of disease and injury depicted or described may also have been prompts to aid the memory of the aspiring surgeon. This hypothesis about a teaching function is given some additional weight by the grouping of the wound-man with several other anatomical figures at the end of the Wellcome manuscript. But the wound-man is also found in other contexts, and sometimes seems to carry a decorative or symbolic meaning, more like a St Sebastian pierced with arrows than a surgical learning device. Very few direct clues are ever found which make clear the wound-man's significance in a particular context.

As we saw in Chapter I, the wound-man illustration was carried over into the printed book in the 16th century virtually unchanged, as were other manuscript forms of medical and surgical illustration. But the coming of the printed book began to affect the ways in which manuscripts were illustrated.

An artist's manuscript model book, which seems to have used printed books as a source, is now in the Department of Prints and Drawings in the British Museum (Fig. 85). It was once part of the Sloane collection, and until 1928 was kept in the Department of Manuscripts. Most of the volume consists of coloured copies of plants in the famous herbal of Leonhart Fuchs, but there are a number of other anatomical, surgical, and mythological illustrations which were almost certainly also culled from printed books. The whole manuscript can tentatively be dated to c.1550. There is a consistency in the manuscript which indicates the work of one hand, and the conjunction of such different subjects suggests that the artist was showing off his expertise rather than pursuing some scientific or didactic purpose. He may have shown this album of paintings in ink and wash to prospective patrons. Scattered through the volume are seven scenes of surgical operations, plus two more of dentistry. In all of the seven scenes the surgeon is dressed in the same puce tunic and red tights, and in all but one he is portrayed as bearded with sandy hair. We must assume that all the surgical pictures came from a single source, not yet identified.

Fig. 85 itself is a picture of the surgeon making an incision prior to an operation for scrotal hernia, captioned in Italian 'El modo de taiar la rotura' ('the method of cutting for rupture'). The surgeon, with his sleeves rolled up in a business-like fashion, makes the first vertical incision necessary to return the abnormal contents of the scrotum to the abdomen. The patient's posture is the most dramatic thing about this picture; he is raised upside down on the board, and bound at arms, chest, and ankles. This position, known as the 'Trendelenburg position' since the late 19th century, in fact goes back to antiquity. An illustration of the same position can be found from the 13th century. It was a sensible arrangement, enlisting the force of gravity on the surgeon's behalf, and making access to the affected area much easier. But in this picture, as in others of the same subject, the angle of the board from the horizontal is much greater than would in practice have been advisable, or even feasible. Probably the artist of this picture, or his model, exaggerated the angle for dramatic effect.

Another feature of this picture worth remarking is the presence of a brazier with two cautery irons. The Arabs refined the basic technique for hernia operations by using a cautery to burn the inguinal canal, in an attempt to stop a recurrence of the hernial descent. It is doubtful whether this, or other such later refinements as the use of gold wire to ligature the scrotal sac, were any improvement on the basic operation, and probably increased the likelihood of subsequent infection (to say nothing of the extra agony for the patient). But it seems that surgical operations for hernias of various sorts were performed by licensed and unlicensed practitioners alike in the Middle Ages, presumably with a reasonable degree of success. A modern commentator has compared the medieval operation to that carried out successfully in modern times by veterinary surgeons.

The artist probably did not care too deeply about the technical details of the operation in any case. His bold and vigorous outline style, combined with flair for dramatic composition and vivid colours, make him better equipped to convey the tension of the scene than the virtuosity of the surgeon's technique. He was not totally in command of the new artistic vocabulary of his day, however – the perspective in the drawing of the surgeon's arm is somewhat shaky.

No survey of medieval surgery would be complete without some mention of dentistry. It was accounted a part of surgery in the Middle Ages, although in the 14th century we find mention of dental practitioners in their own right. Because of the diet, and lack of knowledge of dental hygiene, people must have had many problems with their teeth. There are graphic accounts in medieval writings of the ailments which could afflict the teeth, though illustrations of dental techniques are rarer. The instruments recommended by Albucasis for extracting, filing, or polishing teeth, or for cauterising the gums, are the most common sort of dental illustration. But sometimes, more for the sake of exploiting the awful fascination of teeth-pulling than in a spirit of instruction, we do find single pictures of dentistry. One such is reproduced here (Fig. 86) — from an encyclopaedia compiled by Jacobus, an English-

ELMODO DETAIARLAROTVRA

man with no known surname, who wrote in the mid 14th century. His encyclopaedia was arranged alphabetically, and borrowed extensively from previous encyclopaedists; the section on dentes (teeth) was taken straight from Book 5 Chapter 20 of the *De proprietatibus rerum* ('On the properties of things') of Bartholomew the Englishman, written during the previous century.

At the opening of the section on teeth there is an historiated initial (Fig. 86) representing a surgeon extracting with the aid of a pair of crossed pincers. The surgeon wears a sort of bandolier decorated with gigantic molars, trophies of his former victims. The image is definitely not realistic in spirit: the patient sits with his legs crossed nonchalantly, while the surgeon pulls. The pliers are probably an authentic touch, since Albucasis illustrates a number of pliers like these, some armed with iron teeth themselves, and all part of the surgeon's armoury of dental instruments. But Albucasis recommended that the patient's head should be placed firmly between the surgeon's knees to gain a good purchase, after the preliminary raising of the gums to get at the teeth.

There is nothing of this however in Jacobus's text, which is more of a natural history of teeth than a surgeon's manual. He discusses the number and formation of teeth, their ailments, and the causes of the ailments. He blames evil humours rising from the stomach, or descending from the brain, or a sharp humour which dwells in the gums themselves, or, finally, tiny worms. The idea that such worms might be responsible for dental troubles seems to go right back to the Egyptians, and it was accepted wisdom throughout the Middle Ages. But the undermining activities of the worms would not perhaps have made such a dramatic or instantly recognisable picture as tooth-drawing.

Fig. 86
The nonchalant pose of the patient who is having a tooth extracted belies the realities of 14th-century dentistry. The pincers on the other hand are real enough. Note the surgeon's trophies.
From the encyclopaedia of Jacobus the Englishman.
BL, Royal MS 6 E VI, f. 503v

DIET, REGIMEN, AND MEDICATION

Medicine in the Middle Ages was understood to have two main branches, the theoretical and the practical. Practice was in turn commonly divided into the science of regulating the healthy body, and that of regulating the sick. The regulatory idea was crucial, because, whether dealing with the sick or the healthy, the physician was guided by his understanding of what was a proper balance of the humours for his patient. He sought either to preserve the balance, or to restore it by his advice and medical intervention. The notion was not one of simple equality between the humours in the body; rather, the balance that was aimed at fluctuated according to a whole range of circumstances, from the patient's diet to the weather or the conjunctions of the planets. The body was thought of rather like a hydraulic machine, and the physician's interventions amounted to a sort of fine-tuning of the body's fluids. This applied particularly to blood-letting, which had been employed from classical times as a means of ridding the body of excessive or corrupted humours and fluids.

Blood-letting at prescribed intervals for the healthy, or as a form of urgent treatment for the sick, was certainly the commonest form of medical intervention in the Middle Ages. A large body of rules and associated blood letting lore accumulated, and was handed down in manuscript form (as well as by word of mouth) from generation to generation. The blood-letting man, with lines indicating the points at which blood should be taken, is found depicted in medieval manuscripts almost as often as the tables of urine glasses. The zodiac man (see p. 54) runs them a close third, and he too has strong blood-letting associations; the influence of the signs of the zodiac over particular parts of the body played a central role in determining the when, as opposed to the where, of blood-letting. This question of where was more hotly debated than the question of where, because so many different factors came into play. The seasons of the year (spring was particularly good), days of the lunar month, even hours of the day, were all potentially significant considerations in deciding when to let blood.

A more highly finished specimen of the blood-letting man than is usually found, painted in England in the 15th century, is shown in Fig. 87. The artist has combined indication lines (painted in red), showing the places where blood is to be let, with captions (in blue) which pick out the parts of the body particularly associated with zodiacal signs. Around the borders of this two-page spread run the names or situations of the veins, along with the specific ailments which blood-letting of these veins will relieve. The man himself, and most notably his face, have had the benefit of the attention of a highly competent miniature painter. One curious feature is the suggestion of cables of muscles or sinew running down from the shoulder to the hand,

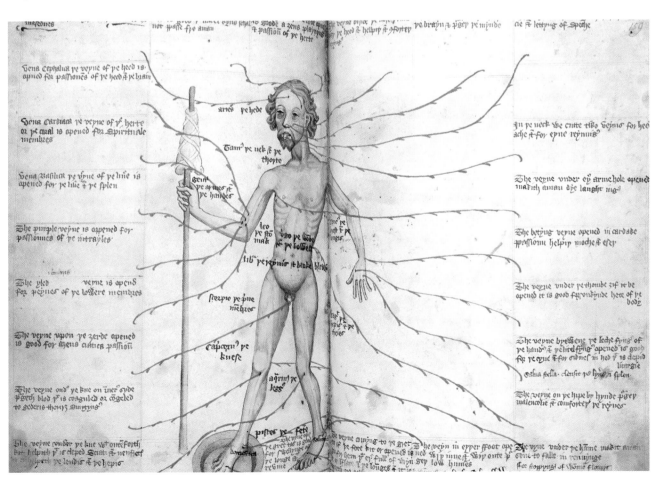

Fig. 87
An unusually fine image of a blood-letting man, spread across two pages, and executed by a professional artist of high calibre. The bowl is presumably to catch blood, but the purpose of the distaff is unknown. From an English 15th-century manuscript.
BL, Harley MS 3719, ff. 158v-159

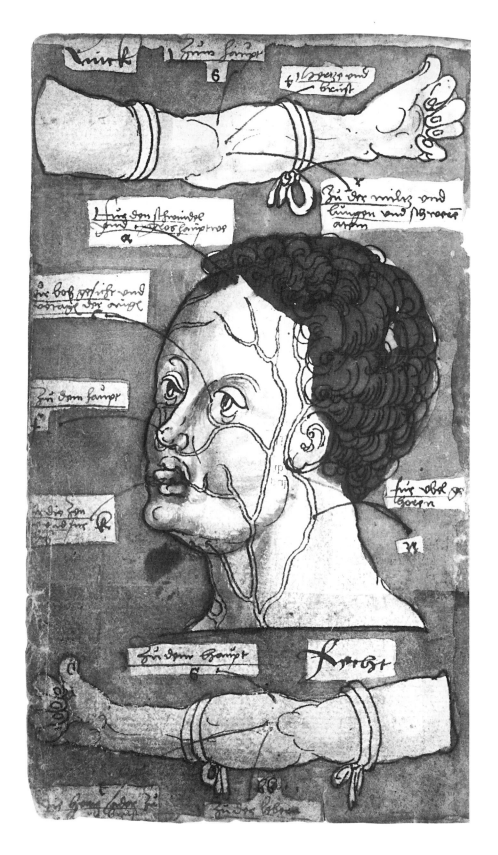

and from the thigh to the foot. In his right hand the man holds a staff, which, by tightening or relaxing the grip, would speed or slow the flow of blood once the arm was incised; the idea of depicting the figure holding a specific sort of staff – a distaff – perhaps originated in some quite different pictorial context, however. The bowl under the figure's right foot no doubt served to catch the blood taken from foot or leg.

It was much more usual to take blood from the limbs than from other parts of the body, except for some illnesses specific to other parts. The most popular of all targets was the basilic vein above the elbow, which the English caption here informs us is 'the veyne of the liver (and there) is opened the liver and the spleen'. Any illness which was diagnosed as local to, or caused by, malfunction in these important organs, would be treated by bloodletting here. The basilic vein was also a good place to take blood generally, because of the role of the liver in the purifying of blood. The very name basilic, deriving from the Greek word for king, indicates the importance attached to this vein. (The picture shows five veins grouped in this upper arm area, all common places for letting blood.) Blood-letting was also used in the treatment of what we would now call mental illness. According to this picture, 'the vein in the nose helpeth the brain and purgeth the mind (of noxious humours)'. In addition, 'the vein under the armhole maketh a man dye laughing'.

Most blood-letting done on a regular basis was quite safe and probably provided psychological reassurance if nothing else, but some of the blood-letting undertaken in the treatment of illnesses very likely did much more harm than good, and must have caused unnecessary deaths in extreme cases.

By comparison with this English 15th-century illustration of blood-letting, a German manuscript of about the mid 16th century shows how the same medical information, contained in a practical handbook, could be presented under new conventions of display. Here (Fig. 88), the artist has concentrated on the head, and the right and left arms. All these members have a more three-dimensional feel

Fig. 88
This page from a German 16th-century manuscript displays blood-letting points on the arms, and the course of the veins on the head. The arm was the most common place for letting blood, and the artist has included realistic depictions of tourniquets on both arms.
Wellcome MS 93, f. 48v

to them – particularly the head, which is modelled with grey wash, and looks like a study from an antique bust. The artist has also made concessions to the new interest in anatomical studies of the age of Leonardo da Vinci and Vesalius. He has tried to trace the paths taken by the veins, though without tackling the problem of individually differentiating and identifying them. In fact this new interest in vein structure is an incongruous partner for the entirely traditional blood-letting text. On the pair of arms illustrated here, the artist reverts to more appropriate conventions and we see the traditional indications for the cephalic, cardiac, and 'purple' veins in the left arm, and the cephalic, hepatic, and cardiac veins in the right. No effort is made here to suggest the course of these veins.

Each of the principal veins in the arm is credited with connection to a major organ – cephalic for the brain, cardiac for the heart, 'purple' for the intestines, hepatic for the liver. Whoever lets the blood would be able to see at a glance which vein to use in order to affect the functions of a particular organ. The same applies to the blood-letting points captioned for the head. All these are cross-referenced by letters of the alphabet to a separate text, which explains the types of disease associated with the organs, and how they may be treated. The emphasis is entirely practical rather than theoretical. When new conventions of pictorial realism are used, as in the portrayal of an arm which is carefully modelled, and not just outlined, realism is made to serve a practical purpose too. So we see the use of tourniquets on the arm, above and below the blood-letting points, as a means of controlling the blood flow.

This manuscript is also of interest for the way it cannibalises some woodcuts, cut out from a printed book. Because woodcuts of zodiac men or tables of urine glasses could be reproduced so quickly in printed books, it was evidently easier for the owner or designer of a manuscript book to borrow such standard illustrations in this way, rather than copy them laboriously by hand. So, by the mid 16th century we have reached a stage where woodcuts – which themselves were based on manuscript models – are beginning to appear as illustrations within manuscript books.

The longitudinal cut in the vein prescribed for blood-letting was not always an easy operation to perform, particularly when undertaken by the ill-trained or inexperienced. There were safer ways of achieving the same result as blood letting, which in incompetent hands could lead to haemorrhage or infection. Cupping was one such safer method. It involved putting heated cups over places on the body where light incisions or scarifications had been made. The blood was drawn out by the vacuum created within the heated cup.

Fig. 89 shows three scenes of cupping from a 15th-century manuscript with English captions. In this case the physician or leech is a woman – and not a menial either. Cupping was a form of medical treatment for which university medical training would hardly have been necessary, and perhaps more appropriate work for a woman than some parts of surgery or general medicine. As we saw in Chapter I, women were not restricted to midwifery, and practised all the branches of medicine in the Middle Ages. But they are not generally seen in medical miniatures practising anything except the ancillary skills of nursing and minor operative procedures – like cupping.

This set of illustrations combines a schematic picture of the different points at which cupping could take place, indicated by the circles on the bodies, and a more realistic idea of the actual art of cupping, with the instruments needed. The patient in the upper picture crouches, holding a staff in front of him. This may be in order to regulate the flow of blood, or is perhaps only for support. To the left of the physician are pictures of two instruments used for making incisions or scarifying. We can see one of them in use in the lower left-hand picture, where the woman seems to be about to incise the patient's thigh. He apparently has his hands tied behind his back, although quite possibly this is simply to allow the artist to give a clear view of his front. The third picture seems to bear this out; the hands on the thighs seem to muddle the design, even if it looks a more natural pose.

Fig. 89
Three pictures showing cupping points (indicated by circles), and a woman applying cups and a cautery. Cupping was used as a less radical means of drawing off blood exploiting the principle of a vacuum within the heated cup. From an English 15th-century manuscript. *BL, Sloane MS 6, f. 177*

Over the page from the pictures in Fig. 89 there is another scene from this series, which differs from the rest in showing cupping of a naked woman patient. Cupping was more often resorted to for women than men, at least by comparison with blood-letting proper. The text that goes with these illustrations, though rather faded and hard to read, notes quite a number of female ailments which can be treated by cupping at the right place, as well as ailments common to both sexes. This text begins by stating that 'cupping above the shoulders purifies the blood generally, stimulates the flow of menstrual blood, and is better for women than blood-letting is'. The points at which the cups are applied, and the sort of ailments which they help to remedy, do not differ much from blood-letting, though obviously cupping was never so practical for the extremities of the body.

We should not take our leave of blood-letting without mention of the humble leech. Leeches were mostly used as an alternative to the other forms of letting blood, but they were sometimes supposed to have qualities peculiar to themselves. Aldobrandino da Siena in his *Li livres dou santé* ('Books of health'), compiled mainly from Arabic authors in the 13th century, suggests that leeches are useful for skin complaints like freckles, acne, or pimples of all sorts. They also help to heal wounds which have been open for a long time. In general they are thought of as ridding the blood of impurities. Aldobrandino also distinguishes carefully between two types of leech, one venomous and the other beneficent, the first frequenting marshes and the second clear running water. He gives instructions that the leeches which frequent clear running water are to be caught the day before use, prescribes how they are to be kept alive, and perhaps most important of all, how they are to be detached – by use of ash, or salt, or other substances with a 'burning' action. Leeches have of course continued to be used, mainly for wound management, right into this century; in fact, a new use has recently been found for them as a way of clearing up tissue after delicate microsurgery operations.

Fig. 90 shows an illustration from the chapter on the use of leeches in Aldobrandino's

Li livres dou santé. We might suppose from looking at this that it was the patient's responsibility to find a stream with fresh-water leeches in it, and paddle up to his knees until they attached themselves. In fact of course the leeches were applied indoors rather than out, and under the supervision of the physician who had them stored in special leech jars. He would make sure that the leeches were applied correctly and in the proper places. The young man sitting rather moodily with his legs in the stream is an indulgence of the artist, functioning only as a signpost to the appropriate chapter of the text. He did not intend to provide a guide to the practice of 'leeching'.

Leechcraft was of course synonymous with the art of the physician, but blood-letting was not the only sort of treatment he had to offer. Like his modern counterpart, the medieval physician did a lot of prescribing of medicines. He did not have the enormous pharmaceutical armoury of the modern Western doctor to draw on, but prescribing was far from a simple matter none the less. The timing of the administration of medicines was of critical importance to the medieval physician, and depended on a number of variables. Of particular significance, as a result of the

Latin translations from Arabic authorities, was the influence of the planets and stars. A good example of this influence is to be found in the *Secretum Secretorum* ('Secret of Secrets'), a text which purports to be an epistle from Aristotle to his pupil Alexander the Great. It is supposed to have been sent to Alexander in the course of his conquest of Persia, because Aristotle was too old to accompany him in person. To people in medieval times, Aristotle was known as 'The Philosopher' and any work of his, including the pseudonymous *Secretum Secretorum*, carried enormous authority, whatever the discipline.

The *Secretum Secretorum* contains advice on statecraft, as one might expect, but it also has a long section on hygiene. A splendidly illuminated copy was written by one Walter de Milemete, clericus, and presented between October 1326 and March 1327 to the young King Edward III, then aged 15, who ascended to the throne in that very year. The book was a particularly appropriate and graceful compliment to the King, not because of its platitudes about statecraft, but because implicitly it put the new King on the same footing as the young Alexander. Naturally such a presentation copy was marked by elaborate

Fig. 91
Doctors attending a king. The doctor depicted at far right holds a laxative herb, prescribed to be taken only when the moon (see top of picture) is in the right house. The king is Alexander the Great. This manuscript, of the *Secretum Secretorum*, was presented to the young King Edward III, in 1327.
BL, Additional MS 47680, f. 54v

illumination, not normally accorded to a manuscript of a secular and practical nature.

Fig. 91 shows the illustration at the head of the chapter on the taking of medicines. We can see the moon with its face peeping out from clouds in the upper left of the picture. It reminds us of the advice of the text to make sure that, when taking a laxative, the moon is in Scorpio, Libra, or in Pisces. The text warns against taking medicine when the moon is in the house of the planet Saturn, for then it will congeal the humours of the body.

The King sits and gestures in a way that suggests the giving, rather than receiving, of advice. Before him stand four doctors, one of whom carries a medicine jar, another a herb (presumably the laxative). By conjoining these symbolic medicinal objects with an equally symbolic moon, the illustrator manages to celebrate the marriage of medicine and astrology, under the auspices of the great King and the great Philosopher.

The prominence of laxatives among the medicines recommended in the *Secretum Secretorum* testifies to the importance of a whole range of purgative medicines in the therapeutic armoury of the time. Purging the body of superfluous or noxious humours was central to the regimen prescribed for sick and healthy patients alike. Many of the herbs and concoctions used must have been drastic in their effects, and vomiting, as much as excreting, was regarded as a natural and beneficial human function, to be encouraged, and where necessary, actively stimulated. But it was recognised that such violent means were not always appropriate, particularly when the patient was aged or weak. The clyster, or enema, was recommended as a less drastic means of achieving the same result, resorted to particularly in cases of constipation. Perhaps as a result of dietary habits, constipation seems to have been one of the commonest ailments for which the medieval patient turned to his doctor for help.

There are some very graphic representations of the clyster-pipe in action in medieval illustrations, and they are often found in the margins of the works of John of Arderne, who wrote specifically on the purposes and practice of clystering. Arderne's approach to the subject was essentially practical rather than theoretical, and the crude diagrams in the manuscripts bear this out. Fig.92 is unusual in that it is a flap of parchment specially stuck on to the page of a manuscript, which had previously been torn. Just visible are the traces of an earlier illustration, now lost, which looks as if it might have involved the clystering of a pig! Nevertheless, this illustrated flap is not just a decorative cover-up for the torn page, but is called for in the text ('as is here depicted', it reads). We see a physician administering a clyster to a patient who seems to be suspended in mid-air; presumably the artist did not feel the need to bother with the cushion or bed upon which the patient would normally crouch or lie, but the effect is to make it look as if the rather apprehensive patient is praying.

Of course what was put in the pipe mattered rather more than the patient's position. Arderne gives one recipe especially adapted for women, children, wounded or fevered men. He prescribes green camomile and wheat bran boiled up together, and then allowed to cool, with the addition of a handful of salt and clear honey or oil. But the basic recipe of salt and water is quite enough for other cases. Arderne says that half a pint of the liquid at most should be used to fill the clyster-bag, which was usually a pig's bladder. The larger end of the pipe should be put into the bladder, and bound fast. The other end of the pipe is anointed with fresh pig's grease, or butter, oil, or honey. With the end of the finger similarly anointed, the pipe can then be introduced into the anus. The bladder is then compressed with the hands. As is stated opposite our figure, if the pipe encounters resistance it should be withdrawn slightly and then re-inserted. Meanwhile the patient should be 'grovelling' above his bed, and rubbing his stomach above the navel with his own hand, or getting someone else to do it for him. He should hold the enema in as long as possible.

Arderne also recommended an improved design of clyster-pipe, a little longer than nor-

Fig. 92
In this marginal drawing in a manuscript of John of Arderne, a surgeon is inserting a clyster-pipe attached to a pig's bladder. Clysters or enemas were recommended by Arderne for a variety of digestive or intestinal problems.
Wellcome MS 550, f. 193v

mal, with the holes placed further up the pipe. We can see the basic outlines of the design even in our little sketch, though some manuscripts show more detailed diagrams of the instrument (see Fig. 82) favoured by Arderne. There are even instructions in the text as to how best to preserve the pig's bladder when not in use (it should be blown up like a balloon, and hung in a shady place.)

It was not only humans who underwent blood-letting, clysters, purges, and medication of all kinds. The horse was an animal of enormous prestige as well as utility in the Middle Ages, and a great number of medical writings devoted to the care of horses were in circulation. The tradition of veterinary medicine in the West goes back to the Greeks, from whom much of the material in the medieval treatises on horse-medicine descended. Two tracts in particular were illustrated – one ascribed to Bonifacio of Calabria, who lived in the 14th century, and one anonymous. These two are found together in a pair of manuscripts, one in the Pierpont Morgan Library in New York, and one in the British Library. The latter manuscript, like the New York manuscript, is in Italian, and probably written and illustrated in the Apulia region of Italy, about 1460 or 1470. It is remarkable both for the artist's concern to display the horse in life-like postures, and for the way in which he has padded out his pictures of horses with grotesques and drolleries. Besides the pictures of medication of horses, there are also equine equivalents of the blood-letting and zodiac men. These performed exactly the same functions for horse medicine as for human.

The horses themselves are depicted in a realistic fashion, sometimes taking medicine through the mouth or nostrils, sometimes being clystered, cauterised or giving blood. Other pictures show various symptoms or external injuries which befall horses. But the creatures which administer the medicines are very often only semi-human, with tails, horns, or cloven hoofs. Others are dwarves or deformed, while both men and women frequently make obscene or insulting gestures. The additional drolleries, found only in these two manuscripts, seem to have been inserted to amuse a particular client, who wanted his therapeutic advice embroidered in this uninhibited and fantastic fashion.

The British Library manuscript was executed by a much more painterly hand than the New York one. Fig. 93 shows a comparatively straightforward scene. A man is administering a medicine through a funnel of horn into the horse's nostrils, while at the same time the horse is being fumigated by smoke from the fire below. The horse's head is tethered to a post – standard practice for this sort of medication. The horse is suffering from a chamorro, a nasal discharge associated with equine strangles or glanders; the author diagnoses an excess of phlegm, which fumigation will counteract. The balance of the humours played just as important a role in horse medicine as it did in human, and the same attempts to get rid of or counteract an excess of any one humour were called for. The medication prescribed here was meant to restore the balance, on just the same principle as that used in treating a man.

Another ingredient of medication in the Middle Ages, whether human or animal, was magic. This element should not be underestimated, since charms are attached to so many of the written recipes which have come down to us; but neither should it be overestimat-

ed, to the extent of thinking that medieval medicine was a lot of mumbo-jumbo to cover up for a lack of rational understanding in therapeutics. Most charms, and doubtless all the invocations to the saints (of whom there was at least one for each part of the body likely to be afflicted), were more like a form of additional insurance, on the principle that no potentially useful agency of healing should be neglected. Written charms nearly always follow detailed recipes, so that both rational and magical means were used together – rather than magic being seen as an alternative to rational medicine.

There was a well-known tradition, probably stemming from the 7th century encyclopaedist Isidore of Seville, that Apollo was the first master of the arts of healing, and that he had disposed of all sorts of magical means. Apollo was to the Christian Middle Ages not

Fig. 93
In this 15th-century Italian manuscript, a horse is being fumigated and medicated for an excess of phlegm, signified by a nasal discharge. Medieval horse medicine was very similar to human medicine in theory and practice.
BL, Additional MS 15097, f. 62v

a pagan god but the earliest and greatest practitioner of many different arts. The first picture of the series of the history of medicine we saw in Chapter 4, is a portrait of Apollo (Fig. 94). According to the caption, 'Apollo healed men with charms and enchantments'. Apollo is seen seated on a highly decorated throne, gesturing towards the open book he holds in his left hand. The book is labelled mysteriously 'the book (that will?)'. Evidently Apollo draws on this mysterious book for his charms and enchantments. Before him stand three patients who all seem to be in a state of trance. They are depicted with their eyes shut, and distinctly off balance, leaning backwards – a kind of levitation may even be taking place. What their ailments may be is not clear. The idea behind Apollo's book may be that there was once a corpus of ancient wisdom on healing kept in book form, which is known only in fragments; we may, it is implied, cherish the hope that the book will one day be rediscovered, and will enable men to recover the lost arts of healing.

Medication of the sick, both by rational and magical means, was only a part of the practice of medicine, and not necessarily the most important part. As we have seen, blood-letting and cupping were also practised as means to preserve health, as well as therapy for the sick. By and large, medical authors in the Middle Ages devoted much more of their attention to ways of warding off illness than their equivalents today amongst Western doctors. No doubt this was partly because faith in the efficacy of their healing techniques in dealing with serious illness was less than the faith we have today. But the Middle Ages also inherited from the ancient world a concern with the effects on health of environment, way of life, and diet, which goes as far back as the Hippocratic school itself. The ubiquitous Galenic physiology, with its central concept of a balance of humours as the preservative of health, only served to concentrate attention still more closely on the factors which might maintain or disturb this happy balance. Because the relative balance of the four humours varied according to the patient's age, sex, station in life, place of living, dietary habits, and regimen, the variables involved in the equation could be very numerous, giving plenty of scope for the professional expertise of the physician.

Those who could afford to consult, or even to have attached to their retinue, a learned physician, were of course usually kings, nobles, wealthy burghers, or eminent ecclesiastics; as

Fig. 94
Apollo, the legendary founder of medicine, seems to have induced a trance in three subjects as a means of healing. He draws his spells from an open book, inscribed 'the book (that will?)'.
BL, Sloane MS 6, f. 175

one might expect, many of the more prestigious treatises devoted to advice on regimen and diet were heavily biased towards the lifestyle of such an elite, and not to the living conditions of the more humble. Not all of the treatises devoted to regimen and health are illustrated, but those that are tend to be illuminated in ways befitting a book intended for the high-born and wealthy. One example in the British Library (see Figs. 90, 95, and 97-99) was composed at the request of Beatrix de Savoie, countess of Provence, in 1256, to take with her on a journey she made to visit her daughters (respectively queens of France, England, and Germany, and countess of Anjou). The author is known to us as Aldobrandino da Siena (see above, p. 98), whose *Li livres dou santé* has the distinction of being the first medical work known to have been composed in French rather than in Latin. (By the time Aldobrandino wrote, French was well on its way to becoming the courtly language of Europe, and it is not surprising that in a treatise intended for a countess, he should have forsaken scholarly Latin for the vernacular.) Aldobrandino, though presumably Italian by birth, seems to have made a successful career in France, and may have even become personal physician to the king. He drew on several Arabic and Western authorities for his text, but particularly on the Canon of Avicenna. His own contribution, besides judicious selection, was to organise his material into sections dealing with health in the body as a whole; in the different members of the body; diet; and physiognomy. Each of these parts is split into a number of chapters, 73 of which, in the British Library copy, begin with an historiated initial. This manuscript, executed towards the end of the 13th century, is the most lavish of all the illustrated copies of Aldobrandino's text, and best accords with a dedication to the countess of Provence.

The initial for chapter eight of book one, on bathing (Fig. 95), has an impressive amount of decoration over and above the picture scene itself. In addition to the usual diaper pattern background to the picture, and the ascender and descender which stem from the main rectangle, we see a man headed dragon at the foot of the initial 'P'. Such marginal fantasies are found even (or perhaps espe-

Fig. 95
Male and female bathers eye each other, at the head of the chapter on bathing in *Li livres dou santé* of Aldobrandino da Siena. This 13th-century miniature is further enlivened by a grotesque growing out of the historiated initial.
BL, Sloane MS 2435, f. 8v

cially) in solemn theological or juristic texts; and this medical book is also enlivened by a select handful of grotesques, as well as a wealth of more ordinary decoration.

The picture itself is a mixture of the medical and the faintly salacious. The two bathers are shown in wooden tubs, which Aldobrandino advocates for bathing in cold soft water. The text also adds that one should not spend too much time in such a bath, only staying to wash off the dirt. The man and woman in our picture certainly do not seem to have their minds entirely on this medical advice – he leers from behind his curtains, while her gesture seems to indicate she is responding to his advances. The text says nothing of mixed bathing, but the bath-house or bagnio of the Middle Ages, where mixed bathing was permissible, was notorious as a place of sexual licence. Nevertheless medicinal bathing had a very long tradition behind it, and was taken seriously, particularly in places with thermal baths, like the famous ones at Pozzuoli near Naples (see Fig. 96).

The text makes an elaborate distinction between different types of water, and discusses their likely effect on the humours, as well as giving some sound advice about not bathing after a meal, keeping oneself warm afterwards, and then eating a light meal of meat. In a classification which goes back at least as far as Galen, bathing was established as one of the 'non-naturals'. The 'non naturals' are not innate, but factors which affect the individual as he interacts with his personal environment. The classical list of six factors was made up of air, food and drink, motion and rest, sleep and waking, secretion and excretion, and accidents of the soul (mental states). Bathing was incorporated in the list by Galen

himself, and often included thereafter. Bathing may be a cause of disease or a preservative against it, depending on whether it is being used properly or improperly.

Aldobrandino also dealt with those factors that we today would call environmental, as well as with purely personal matters like bathing. Chapter 26, for instance, is entitled 'How to know which towns are best to live in' (see Fig. 97). The factors which are important here are whether the town is situated towards the east, north, west, or south, whether it is high up or low-lying, and whether the ground is stony, dry soil, or marshy. Our illustration shows a pair of men entering a town (signified by a crenellated wall with a porch) and, below, three men leaving a similar town. One of these last has his head supported on one hand, and they all seem to be slightly downcast by comparison

with the pair above – perhaps they have chosen to live in the wrong town, and are now suffering the consequences.

Medieval towns were of course fertile breeding-grounds for epidemics of many kinds, and this was sufficiently recognised at the time. Measures to deal with such things as disposal of sewage and butchers' waste were enacted by municipal authorities all over Europe in the Middle Ages. However, medical theory did not have the concepts which could explain how diseases were caused or spread, and most otherwise unexplained outbreaks of sickness were attributed to corruption of the air. According to Aldobrandino, corrupt air could be responsible for fevers, abscesses, eye diseases, and many other illnesses which cause men to die suddenly. Within half a century or so of this particular manuscript having been copied, the shortcom-

Fig. 96
Four bathing scenes from Pietro da Eboli, *De balneis Puteolanis*, a13th-century manuscript from south Italy. These are much more decorous images of bathing, making use of the mineral waters of southern Italy for health purposes only. *Rome, Biblioteca Angelica, MS 1474, ff. 11-14*

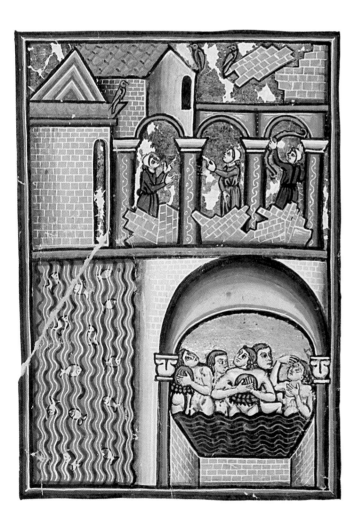

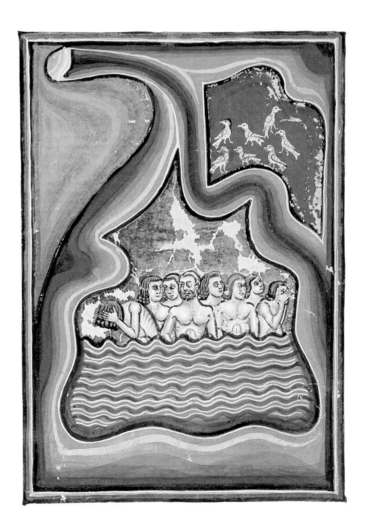

Fig. 97
Advice as to which towns were healthy, and which not, was potentially very valuable in an age when the physical situation of a place was thought to predispose its inhabitants to the great scourges of plague, leprosy, or epilepsy. From Aldobrandino da Siena, *Li livres dou santé*, late 13th-century. *BL, Sloane MS 2435, f. 25*

ings of the medieval understanding of disease mechanisms were to be exposed cruelly throughout Europe by the Black Death. Despite an enormous literature of treatises telling the individual and the community how to protect themselves against the pestilence, which was generally assumed to be caused by corrupt air, nothing could avert or even contain the spread of the Black Death.

The third book of Aldobrandino's treatise is devoted to diet, a subject taken even more seriously then than today. Diet goes hand in hand with regimen in the battle to maintain the precarious balance of the humours, or restore the balance once lost. Food and drink, like the complexion of man himself, are seen as a compound of the basic qualities, either hot and wet, hot and dry, cold and wet, or cold and dry. Those whose complexions are extremely hot and dry would do well therefore to avoid foods which could only exacerbate these qualities, and the same goes for the other combinations. The situation was complicated by the further classification of each of the complexions by degrees, first (or least) up to fourth (or most).

Fig. 98
The miniature at the head of the chapter on pork in *Li livres dou santé* is based on calendar illustrations for the month of November, depicting the killing of the fatted hog. *BL, Sloane MS 2435, f. 46v*

The foods dealt with by Aldobrandino include cereals, meat, vegetables, fruits, fish, herbs, milk products, and spices. Fig. 98 shows the scene at the head of the chapter on pork. Our illustrator is particularly good at capturing a life-like quality in animals, even when his subject is their dead meat. He drew extensively on non-medical sources, bestiaries, encyclopaedias, even works of scripture or devotion, for his models. The pig illustrated here is clearly drawn from the 'occupations of the months' series of illustrations which commonly accompanied the calendars of sacred books. The man hitting the fatted hog with the back of an axe was a favourite theme for the month of November (when animals were killed and the meat stored with preservatives). The text informs us that the domesticated hog's flesh is cold and moist, whereas by comparison that of the wild boar is warm and dry. The younger the pig the colder and wetter its meat, and the more likely it is to engender bad humours; it should only be eaten by those with strong stomachs and of a warm and dry complexion. Otherwise the consumer risks gout in the feet, hands, and legs, or may suffer from the stone, paralysis, and various other ailments.

As well as the whole range of foods, Aldobrandino also includes a discussion of drinks, which, like the foods, interact with the complexion of man. Wine, for example, is distinguished by its quality of heat, although the degree of heat varies with the type and age of the wine. According to Aldobrandino, the warmest wines are those which are clear and reddest; but the slightly less warm, which are 'black' and 'heavy', tend to swell the stomach, and obstruct the passages of the heart. There is a silver lining however – these 'black' wines are good for stopping diarrhoea. Aldobrandino recommends wines which are neither too new nor too old, and his overall verdict is that wine, taken in moderation, fortifies the natural heat of the body, nourishes, makes man joyous, aids nature in its course, and delays the onset of old age.

This encouraging view of wine's medicinal properties is not altogether the theme of the illustration for the chapter on wine (Fig. 99), which shows a monk-cellarer surreptitiously helping himself to wine straight from the barrel. The artist here has caught wonderfully the slyness of the monk, with his stooping posture and his expression of guilty enjoyment. This tone of mockery of the regular orders of the clergy is often found in border illustrations of manuscripts of this period. Here it is transposed to the main picture element but still in the same spirit of gentle fun. There is of course no mention of monks or cellarers in the text! No matter how impeccable the medical credentials of the text, in the age of the custom-made manuscript the illustrator often chose to indulge his own or his client's fancy.

Fig. 99
A monk-cellarer surreptitiously helps himself to a bowl of wine while filling the flagon.
From *Li livres dou santé*, late 13th-century.
BL, *Sloane MS 2435, f. 44v*

107

SELECT BIBLIOGRAPHY

This bibliography is confined to books that should be reasonably easy to find in a good library; it is not meant to act as more than a guide to further reading. In particular I have not listed any of the specialised manuscript catalogues which are the starting points of research into medieval medicine. One such work is L.Thorndike and P.Kibre, *A Catalogue of Incipits of Mediaeval Scientific Writings in Latin* (Mediaeval Academy of America, 1963). The best introduction to medieval medicine is now Nancy G. Siraisi, *Medieval & early Renaissance medicine: an introduction to knowledge and practice* (Chicago, 1990). George Sarton, *Introduction to the History of Science*, Carnegie Institute Publications 376 (Baltimore, 1927–1948), 3 vols. in 5, is the indispensable means of finding out about important writers on medicine and surgery from the ancients to 1400.

On medical illustration there are three important works: Robert Herrlinger, *History of Medical Illustration from Antiquity to A.D. 1600* (London, 1970), and Loren C. McKinney, *Medical Illustrations in Medieval Manuscripts*, Publications of the Wellcome Historical Medical Library, n.s., 5 (London, 1965), and John E. Murdoch, *Album of Science: Antiquity and the Middle Ages* (New York, 1984), which deals with scientific illustration as a whole, including medicine. Three specialised areas of medical illustration are better served than most. There is an excellent set of surgical illustrations in P. Huard, M. D. Grmek, *Mille Ans de Chirurgie en occident; ve – xve siècles* (Paris, 1966). See also the interesting Anglo-Norman series in Tony Hunt, *The medieval surgery* (Woodbridge, 1992). Anatomical illustration is the subject of J. L. Choulant, M. Frank, *History and bibliography of anatomic illustration* (New York, 1945). There are some beautiful plates based on medieval manuscripts in W. Blunt, S. Raphael, *The Illustrated Herbal* (London, 1979).

C. H. Talbot, *Medicine in medieval England* (London, 1967) is an excellent introduction to the writers and scholars of English medicine. S. Rubin, *Medieval English Medicine* (Newton Abbot, 1974) is particularly interesting on the archaeological evidence, and on religious documents as a source of information about medicine. Edward J. Kealey, *Medieval Medicus* (Baltimore and London, 1981) examines the expansion of medical services in England between 1100 and 1154. The later period is dealt with by Carol Rawcliffe, *Medicine & Society in later medieval England* (Stroud, 1995). For information on medical practitioners, see C. H. Talbot, E. A. Hammond, *The medical practitioners in medieval England: a biographical register*, Publications of the Wellcome Historical Medical Library, n.s., 8 (London, 1965). This is supplemented by Faye Getz, 'Medical Practitioners in Medieval England', *Social History of Medicine*, 3 (1990).

Much of the pioneering work on medieval medical manuscripts and their illustration was done at Leipzig by Karl Sudhoff and his pupils in the first three decades of this century. Sudhoff's *Studien zur Geschichte der Medizin* and *Archiv für Geschichte der Medizin* are still valuable, and include more illustrations of medieval manuscripts than any other source. Now ground-breaking work is being done by Helen Valls, a first instalment of which may be found in 'Illustrations as abstracts: the illustrative programme in a Montpellier manuscript of Roger Frugardi's Chirurgia', *Medicina nei Secoli*, 8 (1996), 67-83. Impressive collections of images from medical manuscripts can be found in M.-J. Imbault-Huart, *La Médecine au Moyen Age à travers les manuscrits de la Bibliothèque Nationale* (Paris, 1983), and in Maria Pasca (ed.), *La Scuola Medica Salernitana: storia, immagini, manoscritti dall XI al XIII secolo* (Electa Napoli, 1988). The Italian journal *Kos: rivista di cultura e storia delle scienze mediche, naturali e umane*, published in Milan from 1984 to 1986, included a gallery of beautiful photographs from medical manuscripts, in Italy and elsewhere.

INDEX OF MANUSCRIPTS

Numbers in *italic* refer to the Figures.